CERI
Centre for Educational Research and Innovation

D1243643

THE UNIVERSITY AND THE COMMUNITY

THE PROBLEMS OF CHANGING RELATIONSHIPS

ORGANISATION FOR ECONOMIC CO-OPERATION AND DEVELOPMENT

The Organisation for Economic Co-operation and Development (OECD) was set up under a Convention signed in Paris on 14th December 1960, which provides that the OECD shall promote policies designed:

- to achieve the highest sustainable economic growth and employment and a rising standard of living in Member countries, while maintaining financial stability, and thus to contribute to the development of the world economy;
- to contribute to sound economic expansion in Member as well as non-member countries in the process of economic development;
- to contribute to the expansion of world trade on a multilateral, non-discriminatory basis in accordance with international obligations.

The Members of OECD are Australia, Austria, Belgium, Canada, Denmark, Finland, France, the Federal Republic of Germany, Greece, Iceland, Ireland, Italy, Japan, Luxembourg, the Netherlands, New Zealand, Norway, Portugal, Spain, Sweden, Switzerland, Turkey, the United Kingdom and the United States.

The Centre for Educational Research and Innovation was created in June 1968 by the Council of the Organisation for Economic Co-operation and Development for an initial period of three years, with the help of grants from the Ford Foundation and the Royal Dutch Shell Group of Companies. In May 1971, the Council decided that the Centre should continue its work for a period of five years as from 1st January 1972. In July 1976 it extended this mandate for the following five years, 1977-82.

The main objectives of the Centre are as follows:

- *to promote and support the development of research activities in education and undertake such research activities where appropriate;*
- *to promote and support pilot experiments with a view to introducing and testing innovations in the educational system;*
- *to promote the development of co-operation between Member countries in the field of educational research and innovation.*

The Centre functions within the Organisation for Economic Co-operation and Development in accordance with the decisions of the Council of the Organisation, under the authority of the Secretary-General. It is supervised by a Governing Board composed of one national expert in its field of competence from each of the countries participating in its programme of work.

Publié en français sous le titre :

L'UNIVERSITÉ
ET LA COLLECTIVITÉ :
UNE PROBLÉMATIQUE NOUVELLE

⁎

Since it was set up in 1968 the OECD Centre for Educational Research and Innovation has attempted to define a number of broad lines of inquiry and experimentation in the field of higher education and to instigate sectoral or global innovation by encouraging experiments and the dissemination of their results. After a number of studies on the concept of interdisciplinarity (1969-70), CERI considered how this concept could be applied in the environment and health sectors (1971-74). This series of studies led to consideration of the regional dimension and the elaboration of a specialised institution model geared to regional needs (Regional Health University, 1975). From 1976 to 1978 the Secretariat carried out a broad survey of the universities of Member countries to discover what relationships they had with their environment (more particularly with their local and regional communities) and to examine the problems linked with the " service to the community" dimension, either through the traditional teaching and research functions or through a new function specifically for that purpose. In February 1980 an International Conference attended by 150 participants from 23 Member countries on "Higher Education and the Community: New Partnerships and Interactions" was organised at the headquarters of the OECD on the basis of the results of that survey, submissions by national authorities, and reports by experts.

Throughout the present report references will be found to the preparatory studies and to this important Conference which attempted to throw light on the general set of problems through a better knowledge of the community's expectations and image of higher education and of the mechanisms and resources it can use to respond to those expectations. Examination of the institutional mechanisms for interaction between higher education and the community and the consequences of that interaction on the functioning of higher education were also the subject of in-depth discussions.

The same central preoccupation has guided us from the Nice Seminar on Interdisciplinarity in 1970 to the OECD Conference in February 1980 and throughout the many international meetings held during that period: underlying all the theoretical and practical problems mentioned, *the basic issue has always been the role and missions of higher education, and in particular of the universities.*

This report, which summarises CERI thinking on this matter, is by no means the final word in the debate.

Also available

POLICIES FOR HIGHER EDUCATION IN THE 1980s (in preparation)

THE FUTURE OF UNIVERSITY RESEARCH (March 1981)
(92 81 03 1) ISBN 92-64-12160-9   78 pages
£3.00   US$7.50   F30.00

INTERNATIONAL JOURNAL OF INSTITUTIONAL MANAGEMENT IN HIGHER EDUCATION. Organ of the IMHE Programme
US$25.00, F120.00 per annual volume of three issues. Orders and submission of contributed articles should be made directly to the Head of the IMHE Programme, OECD/CERI, 2 rue André-Pascal, 75775 Paris CEDEX 16.

Prices charged at the OECD Publications Office.

THE OECD CATALOGUE OF PUBLICATIONS and supplements will be sent free of charge on request addressed either to OECD Publications Office, 2, rue André-Pascal, 75775 PARIS CEDEX 16, or to the OECD Sales Agent in your country.

CONTENTS

PREFACE

One crisis can conceal another...

In most of the industrialised countries thinking about higher education, and especially about the universities, concentrates almost exclusively on analysis of the effects of the economic crisis.

This preoccupation is justified:

- the growth in student numbers seems to have stopped in almost all OECD Member countries. Even in countries where it continues — because of the demographic trend and the relatively slow development of the universities in earlier years — there is a decline in unit expenditure per student;
- university budgets have been cut back, sometimes considerably;
- research policies concentrate in the main on the development of new capacities for participation in technological and industrial innovation and neglect fields which have no immediate impact on the economy;
- at the same time, because of the cutback in resources, poor employment prospects for graduates, and the change of emphasis in research, the universities are tempted to adopt defensive attitudes. They are abandoning long-term experiments and perspectives and thus turning away from the broad movement to reform and innovations which had accompanied growth, and simply looking for the most effective ways of adjusting to the new situation in which they find themselves.

Preoccupation with the effects of the economic crisis means that attention is focused only on the impact of general economic trends, that university problems are viewed only as consequences of a recession and therefore cannot be blamed on higher education and it is forgotten that the university during the period of growth itself was shaken by a crisis the root causes of which have not yet been remedied, or even completely understood.

Paradoxically, the economic crisis has silenced a large number of fundamental criticisms that had been made of the university. For reasons unrelated to the crisis, however, it has lost a large part of its monopoly of higher education; research is increasingly being done by specialised institutions or the laboratories of large firms; the university is still not clear how it should bring separate disciplines together to study the great problems of our societies; the growth in student numbers has not brought about democratisation.

The prominent place accorded to the consequences of the crisis must not be allowed to mask the institutional inertia of the university and prompt expressions of respectful sympathy with an *alma mater* which is exposed only to external threats and whose capacity to survive one can only admire.

The authors here adopt a resolutely different attitude. Without neglecting the effects of the economic context and the risks they entail, they deal with the efforts of the universities — and there is a long history of such efforts stretching back to the setting up of the Land Grant Colleges in 1862 — to maintain and rediscover their social

7

significance. In doing this, they link up with the thinking about the significance of the crises of the sixties and seek to identify the mechanisms and types of interaction with its environment which will enable the university to regain the social legitimacy which it was formerly acknowledged to possess.

The book was written on the responsibility of the Secretariat by Guy Berger of the Université de Paris VIII, Consultant, and Pierre Duguet of the Centre for Educational Research and Innovation.

J.R. Gass
Director
Centre for Educational Research
and Innovation

Introduction

A NEW DILEMMA FOR HIGHER EDUCATION

In the sphere of higher education doubts and perplexity have taken the place of the optimism which, it seems, prevailed throughout the 1960s, and which was based on the assumption of its continuous expansion. The optimism was twofold. There was the quantitative aspect (expansion), and the confidence that that expansion would automatically bring about a certain democratisation of our university systems. The outstanding example of such optimism was the paradigm developed by Martin Trow of transition to "a higher education for the masses" and to an age of "universal higher education".

It has, however, since become clear that the American model has signally failed to achieve general adoption in the other industrialised countries. Growth prospects are either non-existent or under severe threat, and education faces fresh constraints because of the almost universal cutback in the funds allocated to higher education. Student numbers are falling — whether because of declining demographic trends, or because of conditions in the labour market and the prospect of persisting unemployment. The recession itself is no longer attributed simply to a cyclical crisis with a predictable end, but to the consequences of technological progress and the change in the amount of labour needed for production activities. It can therefore be assumed that this is no temporary downturn but a profound reversal of trends requiring perhaps an " agonising reappraisal".

We have nonetheless started from the assumption that within the crisis we are now experiencing a new dynamic is already at work to change the position of universities and higher education in general in the economic, cultural and social system, and more especially the role that these institutions play in their immediate environment — whether in the framework of regional policies or not.

The bases for this assumption are:

- an analysis of the changes, real and apparent, that have taken place in higher education over the last 20 or 30 years, chief among these being the growth in student numbers on the one hand, and a number of crises (the most noteworthy being that of 1968) which were linked to a combination of general social problems;
- recognition of the new circumstances facing higher education: the cutback in resources, and in particular the impossibility of making any plans for development and expansion;
- observation of a number of experiments prior or subsequent to the economic downturn which, though far from typical of what is happening in the majority of institutions, indicate a new approach to defining the aims of higher education.

Development in terms of growth and wider access

During the period of growth substantial changes certainly occurred in higher education, but they were by and large confined to non-university institutions. In some countries indeed there was even talk of introducing a binary system. Apart from the setting up of a few experimental institutions, the universities themselves resisted change, and in some cases reacted to the introduction of a new peripheral system by reinforcing their own traditional characteristics.

The universities accepted the large-scale recruitment of new teaching staff and the introduction of administrative machinery and management structures slightly better suited to the demands of growth. But their foremost concern was to provide access for more students from a broader social spectrum whilst at the same time ensuring that the structures, methods and content of the education they offered were conceived and organised just as before, in accordance with their basic task: the production and transmission of knowledge.

That is precisely the reason why *this study will deal essentially with the relations between the university and the community.* The universities still constitute the central structure of higher education. Their resistance to change makes them especially vulnerable to the present crisis. The possibility of a new dynamic thus seems particularly significant for them. Further on we shall see how the very concept of the university differs from one country to another, depending on the balance prevailing between the central system and university institutions, and also even within a given country, depending on the local circumstances of particular universities. In this introduction therefore we can only provide a global approach to the question.

As far back as 1973 the possibility of a change in the goals of higher education was discussed at length in international conferences held at the OECD on the future structures of post-secondary education. There it was considered that, in addition to providing for the transmission and extension of knowledge, modern systems of post-secondary education should also:

— play an important role in the general social objective of achieving greater equality of opportunity;
— provide education adapted to a great diversity of individual qualifications, motivations, expectations and career aspirations;
— facilitate the process of lifelong learning;
— assume a " public service function", i.e. make a contribution to the solution of major problems faced by the local community and by society at large, and participate directly in the process of social change.

The first three of these " new goals" concern the extension of the student population, and adapting education more fully to its diversity — still really part of the function of the production and transmission of knowledge. Only the last, therefore, can properly be said to be something really new.

But even then, this direct participation in social development, though encouraged, was regarded with suspicion. This is clear from a study commissioned by the OECD on the new universities, where an ironic tone fails to conceal some sense of alarm: " The competition between all types of organisations from political parties to interior decorators to have as many professors as posible on their advisory boards or as speakers at their meetings may be an amusing sidelight rather than a warning signal. What seems more important is the high and increasing degree to which university professors in a wide range of disciplines are called upon by public and private parties for expert opinions, consultation and special research assignments, a development which again is viewed with increasing concern since it tends to lead to neglecting the regular academic functions" [1].

Most of the action taken recently in regard to higher education in the OECD countries (and in fact almost everywhere, including the socialist states and the developing countries) has focused largely, or sometimes exclusively, on the goals of generalisation and democratisation of access. In almost every case the purpose has been to regulate access more effectively in the light of employment, make more efficient use of both human and material resources, develop opportunities for continuing training, foster the mobility of students from short technical courses to long courses and vice versa, and reduce the social costs and the frustration caused by drop-outs. This trend has been reflected in the increase in new universities as part of a more effective network, and the grouping together of institutions providing short and long courses (for example, Gesamthochschule in Germany, integration of the IUTs into the universities in France, multi-campus universities in the United States, the Swedish reform). Concurrently, certain new institutional structures have come into being, such as the Universities without Walls in the United States and the Open University in the United Kingdom.

It was almost inevitable that an approach centred mainly on access, employment prospects and a more efficient performance in the training sector would show up contradictions and generate conflicts that would tend to accentuate certain aspects of the crises in the universities, or indeed provoke new ones.

It is in fact difficult to tackle problems of access, regulation of employment and educational performance simultaneously. To make access available to everybody either automatically means increasing problems for graduates when they leave or courting an intolerable drop-out rate. Regulating access in the light of employment possibilities, apart from its technical difficulties, means giving up democratisation and agreeing that higher education is still the privilege of the few. Admittedly, the demand for education is now being virtually stabilized but, apart from the fact that nobody knows how long the relaxation of social pressure is likely to continue, the level of stabilization is sufficiently low in most countries to make it impossible to speak of any real equality of opportunity, but it is high enough to produce an imbalance between the numbers of graduates and the jobs available for them.

Trying to fulfil both obligations simultaneously (that is, to satisfy demand for access to higher education and to regulate it strictly in line with labour market conditions) means accepting, as some countries have done, that student failures and dropouts are the only means of regulation available to university administrations, however perverse and underhanded that may be. For countries in which this happens, this would explain some aspects of the lack of interest in efforts to improve university teaching.

Above all, this regulation of access/future employment approach focuses too much attention on the training function, making the university consider only one aspect of its social objectives — teaching and the production of graduates. This has led to a twofold conflict.

There is a conflict within the university system itself, since it is compelled to choose between its vocations as a producer of graduates and as a producer of knowledge, and is increasingly coming to consider research as the sphere in which it can exercise autonomy, while the training function represents its social dependence.

But above all there is a conflict between the university and society. Whether the aim is to satisfy social demand or to organise training in the light of available employment, the traditional relations between the university and the community are invariably formulated in terms of the university's subordination to the community, not in terms of interaction and co-operation. This only accentuates their failure to get on together, and leads the university to strive for an autonomy that sometimes amounts to isolation.

11

Fundamental reform: essential, but impossible in current economic circumstances

Many of these changes we have been considering, almost all of which are purely institutional, have still not provided answers to the problems that triggered off the student revolts in the 1960s.

It can surely not have been forgotten that in 1964 the Berkeley campus of the University in California was the starting point for a wave of student unrest that shook universities in many countries with a violence that reached its peak in 1967 and 1968 in Berlin, Paris, Tokyo and Mexico City. The origins and development of these student movements were very varied: students at Berkeley in 1964 wanted to use the campus for political action; at Columbia in 1968 the protests centred on the University's research contracts with the Defense Department, and the conversion of a park in Harlem into a stadium for student use. Other examples were the attacks on Axel Springer's press empire (Berlin, 1967), demonstrations against Japan's dependence on the United States and opposition to tuition fees (Tokyo, 1968), and the campaigns in French universities for students to have the right to receive other students of the opposite sex in their hostels — and for freedom of political expression within the university (Antony, 1965 and Nanterre, 1968).

But although the revolts were nearly always triggered off by matters unrelated to the operation of the university system, and although their origins and the forms that they took differed widely on account of varied social and political circumstances, what was really surprising was the international character of the crisis. The organisation and methods of higher education differed, and still do, not just from one country to another, but in some cases from one university to the next. In spite of this, some common features were present, and some of the factors at work were identical in every country, namely changing attitudes among the young, and the teaching system's failure to adapt to new requirements.

These explain the protests against fragmented knowledge spread over an infinite number of self-contained specialities, protests against the compartmentalisation in universities which shields them from social, economic and political realities, organised resistance to a type of teaching that is often scholastic and abstract, the rejection of training courses that are too strictly circumscribed and inconsistent with the realities of working life, the realisation of the growing disparity between qualifications and actual job requirements, and the refusal of students to accept a status often involving an intellectual and social dependence which effectively rules out any creative activity or personal commitment.

These protests can only be regarded as justified today when we look at employment trends and the way in which many universities have reacted to the cutback in their resources. Their reactions are inevitably defensive:

— preserving what they regard as the essentials, i.e. research in its traditional forms, the "academic" disciplines, and the development of critical thinking in general;
— attempting to do "what the university is there for" as best they can, under difficult conditions, at the expense of trying to develop new functions; in short, accepting the risks of abandoning, for the time being at least, any experimental or innovative approaches;
— increasing resistance to social pressures, which are themselves increasing because of the desire to control the use of resources that have become scarce.

New relations between the university and the community: the key to fundamental reform?

The present study is a reconsideration of a policy that has so far concentrated too much on the question of access — its extension, diversification or limitation — and on the problems arising from it such as organisation of teaching, recruitment of teaching staff, degrees, and qualifications.

In supporting an approach that is less concerned with the quantitative expansion or decline of the universities and not solely preoccupied with their teaching function, we feel that we are recognising the major importance of the democratisation of higher education and the social and economic development higher education can stimulate. At the same time we are also concerned with the new objectives of higher education, and hence with finding answers to the questions raised in the foregoing discussion.

The problem of democratisation brings up the question of a university's social function in the very broadest sense of the term. It includes not only the development of access to qualifications but the production of knowledge, and the social significance of that knowledge. It also involves a change in the sharing of responsibility for the development of knowledge and teaching.

Even in the present situation is a number of trends that may be regarded as positive. A widespread conviction seems to be developing in all countries that if its research and training functions are to be properly performed the university must become part of its environment ("environments" would be more accurate) and develop its capacity to influence and benefit that environment. It is increasingly felt that a university should be able to draw upon existing competences wherever it finds them, and disseminate information wherever it is needed. If the university is to be effectively integrated into the community it must no longer concern only those who attend the university, namely the teachers and the students. It should be possible to pass on one's skills without being a teacher, and to receive training without being a student.

Above all, it is increasingly felt that a university should not respond to demands from the community with *a priori* models based on theoretical expectations, and consider the community merely as a field of application; it should, rather broaden its concept of research and constantly realign its theoretical models on current, concrete situations. This presupposes a new definition of the environment of higher education institutions, a new balance between functions, a new type of interaction between these institutions and the community or communities that form their environment, of which the training of students is merely the most apparent aspect, calling for the largest share of resources.

One of the central tasks, therefore, is to make clear what we mean when we refer to the university's "environment" and the "community". Should we confine ourselves to a geographical and geopolitical framework, making an inventory of all the university's possible partners, and listing a number of target populations or goals? While the concept of the university is relatively clear and amenable — though with enormous difficulty — to international comparison, the definition of the community raises major problems and will in fact depend on the type of relationship envisaged in each separate set of circumstances.

Questions, and some tentative answers

To examine the validity of these assumptions, and to identify their consequences for the structures and functions of the university is the main purpose of the body of this study. The scope is accordingly limited, for our focus throughout will be on the university system, not the communities and social groups with which the universities are linked.

During the survey on which this monograph is based (and this included the preparation of special studies, conferences and meetings of professional people concerned) particular care was taken to obtain informed opinion and data bearing upon the following questions:

i) Is there a real and significant increase in the community-oriented activities of the university?

ii) Can this increase be interpreted as reflecting a qualitative change in the relation between the university and the community: is it a new trend, or simply an extension of the tradition of " service" found in many institutions?

iii) Does this movement reflect a desire on the part of the universities themselves to turn to their environment in order to act upon it or draw more resources from it, or is it determined by pressure from the environment, or finally does it reveal a new permeability between higher education and society? In other words, what is the balance between the internal dynamic and external pressures? How great is the risk of treating what may be a genuine social innovation simply as a new pedagogical tactic?

iv) Whatever the final significance of this trend, has it any significant impact or fall-out on the structure of higher education, accepted teaching practices, the ideological models disseminated by the university, or the status of academic staff or students?

v) If we can speak of change, is this confined to certain sectors of university activity, involving a few specific disciplines or groups of disciplines such as health, education, technology, the environment, or is there a general change, uneven perhaps in its incidence, but affecting most disciplines and sectors of activity?

vi) In almost all countries there is an evident crisis in knowledge, or rather a breakdown of general confidence in scientific and technical progress. Could a new interpretation of the relations and reciprocal duties of the university and the community lead to an amelioration of this uneasy situation, perhaps by enabling a revised conception for the future roles of science and technology?

All these questions derive from the observable fact that the great difficulties experienced in higher education in almost all Member countries over the last ten to fifteen years, and the bringing into question of the university's place and social value, are all connected with the type of relationship the university has with the community and its immediate or general environment. It will be seen, too, that they are based on the assumption that changing that relationship is an essential element in solving the persistent difficulties.

In the light of the clarification of issues by the survey carried out by CERI 1976-79 and subsequent professional discussions, in particular at the International Conference of February 1980, the findings and proposals of this project are grouped around four main themes, as presented in Parts One to Three and the concluding chapter in the present volume.

Part One deals with the definition of the university's environment. It identifies and criticises the various accepted senses given to the concept of " service", and indicates a number of more or less implicit strategies for the development of relations between the university and the community.

To provide an empirical background for all the issues, Part Two describes a number of working arrangements, either institutional or informal, at national or " local" levels. These arrangements by no means reflect the variety of existing situations and responses, and represent only a small part of the data collected. They are cited simply to provide a basis for a set of questions, not a full picture of the current situation.

Part Three deals with the consequences — for the institution, for teaching and for research — of providing access to new types of populations, and of the emergence of new practices, new content and a new type of university teacher, and the risks involved in making changes in a traditional system of values based on objectivity and scientific method.

The final chapter, Conclusion, deals with the confrontation between university independence and the responsibilities entailed in full acceptance of its cultural, social and economic role. As interaction develops it is bound to affect the internal equilibrium and operation of higher education. The more universities turn to their environment, the more they themselves will be subject to the strains and conflicts that affect society in varying degrees. How then are the traditional values of independence, objectivity and universality to be reconciled with the assumption of greater responsibility for the problems of the community, whether cultural or economic? What impact will this new commitment have on the way higher education works? How can the critical faculty be safeguarded and strengthened in the context of this practical commitment; how can objective scientific values themselves be made an instrument of social change?

A new conception of the democratisation of higher education

As the study of students' social origins has shown, and in spite of the appreciable growth in the representation of less-privileged social groups, the question of the democratisation of higher education cannot simply be reduced to a question of access. Although the generalisation of primary and secondary education systems has been a vital factor in their democratisation — though the process is far from complete, since there too access alone is not enough — the question cannot be put in the same terms for higher education and the universities, and the " democratisation of higher education" cannot be regarded as something that will follow simply from the increase in student numbers and the transition from "universities for an élite" to "higher education for the masses".

Taken as a whole, the cases analysed seem in fact to show that the development of relations with the community leads to a qualitative break reflected in the following changes:

The emergence of a new category of students who, in the context of continuing education or even of basic training courses, are enrolled as full university students even though they continue in occupational employment and may not even hold the qualifications for university entrance (secondary school leaving certificate).

In coming to terms with their environment some universities have systematically addressed specific population groups — manual workers, migrants, women, elderly persons, ethnic minorities, and people living in economically or culturally backward areas — offering them general or special training directly connected with their immediate needs or particular cultural and social practices.

In some cases the university has gone out to the population groups it wished to reach; in other cases a new population group has come on to the campuses and into those monuments of élitist culture which European universities used to be.

The second notable change seems to be that, increasingly, attending university does not always mean taking a full course leading to a degree. Situations of this kind are found in all countries. This drastically changes the numbers and types of students, and reflects the fact that universities are increasingly providing " initiation" courses as well as their normal degree courses. This means an increase both in the range of subjects and the number of levels at which they are taught, and gives rise to other problems.

A third change seems to be the emergence of what we shall call " collective subjects" [2]. Education, especially at higher levels, has traditionally been directed at the individual whose advancement was ensured by the award of a certified qualification.

15

Now, through its relations with the local or regional environment, the university is increasingly obliged to deal with interest groups, associations, professional bodies and company workforces. The demand for training in these cases is often connected with community action in spheres such as town planning, pollution control, work organisation, the response of a minority group to a conflict situation, or a collective artistic production.

The democratisation of higher education is a question of the right of access for all to the resources both material and intellectual of higher education. It would seem wrong to consider the exercise of such a right on an individual basis only (individual course — individual certified qualification) for what is in fact a collective good and a collective product. In any case there is no such thing as a demand for universal access as students to universities.

All these changes thus give a most substantial shift to the commonly accepted meaning of "democratisation of higher education". Instead of this meaning simply an increase in numbers of students and hence of graduates, or the introduction of selection methods putting less emphasis on cultural and social backgrounds, we see the emergence of a variety of schemes for putting all the university's facilities at the disposal of the whole population, but without making everyone into students and potential graduates. This seems to us to be a major change whose impact has not yet been properly assessed.

Graduates and new knowledge are not the university's only outputs

It is hardly surprising that the university should tend solely to reproduce itself and to reproduce society when the only relations it has with its environment are at the beginning and at the end of the courses it provides — that is, on intake, when the financial resources available and the flow of students on which they are spent are decided, and at the output end when the university's "products" (knowledge and graduates) are distributed throughout the social system, for the latter to use as best it can. Universal access to the resources of higher education means a different ordering of its priorities and above all the establishment of a profoundly different relationship with its environment.

As the development of the social sciences has confirmed, the university must be regarded as a complex system which can only function and be understood through its relations (dependence, exchange, resistance, transformation) with its environment.

So long as these interactions are kept to a minimum it is extremely difficult to establish a balance between the different branches of university activities — scientific (production of knowledge), economic (producing qualified cadres and workers and contributing to the development of production), and socio-cultural (development of persons and groups, production of values, and the like).

In such conditions the university system is consistently distorted to the benefit of one or other of these branches of activity:

— Development of knowledge for its own sake, which tends to turn the university in on itself in an indefinite process of self-reproduction;
— Excessive devotion to the occupational needs of the economic system, and subjection to existing socio-economic structures and the dominant forms of production;
— Perpetuation of the aristocratic cultural myth according to which the university bestows a general culture on a varying number of individuals, for them to use as they wish or simply as they are able because of their membership of a particular social group.

The right balance cannot, in our view, be achieved by any change, however far-reaching, in the internal structures of the university. *The only way it can be done seems*

16

to be by reorganising the exchanges the university has with its environment, i.e. by introducing a new type of interaction with the community.

This does not mean that, in some combinations of circumstances, a refusal to yield to social pressure and the development of particular values, especially at a time when they are no longer universally accepted, may not be the most pertinent and most urgent service that the university can perform. But even the phenomenon of the " ivory tower" must be understood in terms of interaction, not as a symbol of an illusory independence.

It may well turn out one day, to borrow a play on words from the Quebec researcher Réal Larose, that "la véritable science de l'école, c'est l'écologie", in other words that education is really about the relations of an individual, a group or a system with its environment.

Pointers for a critical examination of relations between the university and the community

We do not intend here to summarise particular cases and tendencies the chief characteristics of which are their diversity and a desire to increase that diversity still further in an attempt to match more fully the scale and complexity of real situations. Instead, we shall propose a number of topics for analysis:

— the differences between the university's view of its role and what the community expects from it;
— a set of possible responses by the university to the demands of the community, which could constitute a first attempt at a taxonomy of university/community interactions;
— the various images the university itself has of the community;
— possible overall strategies that would determine the choice of the main lines on which interaction and institutional mechanisms could develop.

Analyses along these lines will, we think, provide us, if not with criteria for evaluation, then at least with some instruments for a critical review of policies so far pursued. These comments may have to be modified in the light of empirical findings from experiments that are still running, but the general views we present here should already be enough to provide a basis for detailed case studies.

At this point we shall confine ourselves to describing four review criteria that seem to us essential. But first we must draw attention to the ambivalence of most of the statements made about university/community relations. The university system, both in function and in structure, is so complex that any form of solution offered raises a new problem. This may appear a truism, yet it becomes important when we bear in mind the resistance — irrational or legitimate — displayed in its various manifestations by both the university and the community. Enquiries carried out for the OECD Conference of February 1980 — E. Bockstael's of trade unionists and industrialists in the United States, T. Umakoshi's of the populations making up the environment of Hiroshima University, or Y. Laplume's of a number of mayors of university towns or chairmen of regional councils in France — all indicate a surprising mixture of enthusiasm and scepticism, of concrete demands and general mistrust. Such resistance is continually fostered by, and adds to, the ambivalence of the findings.

There are always two ways of interpreting the establishment of closer links between university and community. This is so whether it is a question of research policies and the inappropriateness of distinctions between fundamental and applied research; or education policies, and the contradictions that arise between the adjustments that are bound to be made to meet the demands and structure of the employment market, and the need to avoid accepting the strait-jacket of vocational training, which would mean losing any ability to adjust; or, finally, the new "service" functions which can acquire new prospects and long-term aims when they take the community into account but can also find themselves giving undue weight to immediately "profitable" objectives. Access to new sources of funding and equipment provides a particularly striking example. Whether for research or training, new resources can increase a university's potential, and hence its autonomy; at the same time, however, they bring the university into the market economy and hence reduce its freedom to "propose" since only "acceptable" and "credible" offers will be taken up.

This ambivalence makes it necessary to specify more clearly the directions in which community-oriented activities must be increased and new institutional mechanisms introduced. They cannot, it would seem, be considered simply as an extension of teaching and research since they both pose a threat to these traditional functions, and also provide a fresh definition of tasks and a new, less self-centred balance for the university. In other words, instead of the closed system arising from the theoretically unlimited expansion of training activities stemming from a desire for greater democracy and the exponential development of knowledge in the name of the independence of science (an expansion subject only to the arbitrary limitation of resources), it is possible to have a systematic policy of developing substantive relations with the environment, forming an open system that is permanently regulated (and hence on occasion controlled) by reactions and proposals emanating from the community.

The first review criterion may accordingly be formulated as follows: is the widening range of community-oriented activities to be considered simply as an extension of teaching and research, developed in fact as a fresh source of funding for these traditional activities, or is it a sign of a change of balance in the university's tasks, and of the introduction of a new, open system of regulation beween the university's pursuit of its own ends and the demands of the environment?

The second review criterion proposed is to determine how far particular methods and strategies are suited to national or local circumstances, that is to economic and political characteristics and to social structures and cultural traditions.

In Part One, Chapter 4 we have listed a number of major indicators — level of development, degree of centralisation, relative weights of government, trade unions and employers' associations, and the like, existence or lack of a regional planning policy, and the "central" or "internal" character of those regional strategies.

To this should be added some sociological indicators such as the extent of social stratification, the value attached to qualifications and academic ability; also the functioning of the local authorities, and the degree of internal democracy in universities and enterprises. Only when criteria of this kind are taken into account can the various working arrangements under consideration be compared one with another, and particular difficulties or dangers of failure or of diversion from objective be understood.

The degree of feasibility of each arrangement, and in particular of each strategy, is the *third review criterion* that can be applied to the various forms of interaction here described. This in turn has to be related to the earlier criteria, on which feasibility in fact depends.

Lastly, a fourth criterion in our view should be how far the proposed change is innovative and capable of interacting with the system as a whole. This should allow the various proposals identified to be reviewed and examined as innovation strategies. In the general social and economic context already described, where experimentation has been brought to a halt almost everywhere, the fact that original relationships between universities and their environment take the form of "local" innovations, highly diversified and not easily reproducible, constitutes one of the few opportunities for innovation.

There can thus be no question of putting forward a model solution that would be

18

introduced in prescribed stages. The experiments here described have an open, uncontrollable timescale, with periods of latency and periods of accelerated movement. We do not claim to be proposing ways of reducing distortion and crisis, and we fully understand that universities may decline to commit themselves to a process that can only be monitored after the event, and may be more inclined to protect their independence than to exercise it.

But after analysing the forms of relationships between the university and the community, a problem encountered at the outset of the crisis crops up again, namely *the dynamic tension set up by the development of new relations, a tension that determines at one and the same time institutional changes, teaching reforms, and reconsideration of the fundamental tasks and the conception of knowledge and its social functions.*

Action therefore cannot simply be oriented in terms of consistency, adaptation or feasibility. The scale of the desired change must also be taken into account. From this point of view, like recurrent education, to which it is in any case closely linked, and which must not be limited to continuing education, the development of new relations with the community may be considered either as a partial policy to deal with a number of specific questions, or as a general and all-embracing approach. Here we have attempted to review the possible consequences, for the conception of the role of the university, of opting for the second approach.

Part One

THE UNIVERSITY'S PLACE IN SOCIETY

Chapter 1

THE UNIVERSITY – IMAGE, STATUS AND ROLE

There seems general agreement on the need for fruitful, two-way co-operation between the university and society, and on the fact that the university stands neither aside from nor above society but forms an integral part of it.

What society could say that it was indifferent to the development of high-level education, refused to recognise the importance of research, and could do without structures for reflection, study and training? Where is the university which would not claim that it is contributing to the betterment of the society to which it belongs, and has always done so, whether by training the citizens of that society or by studying what must be done to improve it? And yet somehow, for reasons not unrelated to the recent expansion of universities which has caused the public to take a much closer interest in their functioning, and more especially the recent discovery that educational expansion by itself is no guarantee of democratisation, nor of social, economic and cultural improvement, and finally, as a direct result of the contraction of resources of industrialised societies and the decline in growth rates, it seems that a climate of mutual mistrust has grown up.

As Jacques Franeau, Rector of Mons University in Belgium so aptly put it: " the university feels it is not well liked by society, and society feels it is not well served by the university". In most of the OECD Member countries, public opinion sees university teaching as inappropriate and sometimes outdated, and university research as over-formal, expensive and rarely leading to discoveries, still less to practical applications. The universities complain that governments and economic forces, and in some cases public opinion as well, always take the short-term view. Society, somewhat illogically perhaps, criticises the university for being an inward-looking community and at the same time criticises university staff and students alike for constantly interfering in matters that do not concern them and expressing opinions on things in which they have no say.

The universities blame society for failing to assign them an adequate proportion of its resources, seeking to control their activities too closely, and not providing suitable outlets for their graduates.

As they have extended and multiplied, universities have become highly complex institutions. To a student entering it for the first time, the university is often a labyrinth at the centre of which some mysterious minotaur is lying in wait for them. Representatives of community groups who in some countries sit on the university governing boards — representatives of local, regional or central authorities, trade union officials, businessmen — are surprised at the complex institutional arrangements and the juxtaposition of structures mutually unaware of each other's existence which only come together to discuss budgets or elect officials. Unlike the vocational colleges and the specialised institutions making up the rest of post-secondary education, it is very hard, even in the case of universities that have existed for centuries, to say exactly what they are and do.

1. SEMIOLOGY OF RELATIONS BETWEEN UNIVERSITIES AND THEIR ENVIRONMENT

The difficulty of identifiying the universities, and the dangers of incomplete perception that this entails, are clearly exemplified in the varied forms of spatial development that they present, the ways in which they are sited, and their physical image generally. This is particularly true since the siting of these institutions, whether for practical reasons or more deliberate ones of policy, has always implicity expressed the educational objectives that the universities have adopted or that society has set for them.

The isolated campus

Strangely enough, the more or less secluded campus and the central university usually standing like a monument in the heart of the city are both manifestations of the same proud independence. The campus originated in the United States. It was only during the 1960s that Europe followed this model of organisation, a model that some countries rejected as a result of the student unrest in 1967-68 which first occurred in this type of university setting. It continues to hold a certain fascination, nonetheless, and is still the preferred model.

The campus is an isolated, self-contained location. It is a kind of monastic refuge where knowledge and wisdom can thrive free of all constraint. The concern for knowledge — and for truth — has always led universities to seek a certain isolation. Research and education are pursued for their own sake. They need no justification: they are an end in themselves. The campus thus finds "its ideological expression in a way of life shielded from any urban contamination. The principle of the campus is separation, not only from the city but also from the rest of the territory, and to make such separation tolerable it was necessary to rebuild an urban microcosm in the country, i.e. a negative of the actual anarchical industrial city, seething with social conflicts" [3].

The new universities established in the United Kingdom during the 1960s — Sussex, East Anglia, Stirling, Essex, Warwick, Ulster, York, Lancaster, Kent — are all examples of this kind of campus, as an OECD study[4] pointed out: " all the sites without exception are in beautiful countryside unencumbered by industrial development, yet all are within easy reach by road, or even on foot, of old-established communities. Unlike the colleges of Oxford, Cambridge, St. Andrews or Durham, they are not intertwined with their small communities, dominating them and their daily activities. Nor are they encapsulated, like the older civic universities, in much larger industrial cities which dominate them. For better or worse they are detached, self-contained entities — villages or, potentially, small towns in themselves — physically distinct from their adjacent communities. All the new universities are "campus" universities on large, self-contained sites. The later ones have benefited from the University Grants Committee's insistence that the promoters should be able to provide a site of at least 200 acres, with sufficient space for all the facilities, including playing fields and some residential accommodation, required by a university of at least 3 000 students, which it considered to be the 'minimum viable size' ".

The same idea of an urban microcosm in a rural setting is to be found in the following description of the site for the new University of Konstanz in the Federal Republic of Germany. "The site on which the university will be built lies just beyond the town gates and will be arranged as a campus, the central idea determining the whole lay-out. On undulating slopes covering a vast area of 200 hectares and bounded by forests, the university will comprise a central nucleus from which the main buildings branch out in the form of a cross the arms of which will be about 350 metres long. The student hostels complex, a veritable rural community, will be a few minutes' walk away, in a small river valley." Needless to say, not all campuses have been established in such Rousseau-inspired bucolic settings, criss-crossed by streams and brightened by birdsong, havens of peace and tranquillity. There are numerous examples of barrack-like campuses surrounded by high-rise blocks of low-cost housing estates or industrial ghettos[3].

An urban setting for a university is also entirely compatible with isolation, and the "monumentalism" of the older European universities and indeed of more recent ones (an echo seems to run from the high-rise tower of Moscow's Lomonossov University to the otwer of the University of Paris VII or that of the University of Constantine in Algeria) may create a symbolic separation as effective as actual distance. The isolation of the urban university from its surroundings is moreover linked with the history of universities. In the Middle Ages the universities of Western Europe were located in city centres, but as enclaves enjoying special privileges in the same way as the guilds or the religious congregations. They acquired autonomy through persistent struggle with the ecclesiastical and temporal authorities. This historical fact, coupled with a particular view of the role and functions of the university, often resulted in isolation.

It is true that location in urban or suburban surroundings, and more generally in a living social and economic fabric, at least has the advantage over the isolated rural campus of making exchanges easier by reducing the physical or psychological barrier of transport, without necessarily removing it altogether. But whether they are "liners in the prairie" or "fortresses in the suburbs", as the universities of Lethbrige in Canada and Bielefeld in Federal Germany have been described by "Architecture d'Aujourd'hui"[3], these isolated campuses effectively remove the danger of "social contamination" in either direction, but may enable the university to sink further into self-reproductive routines.

The dispersed university

It should not be assumed that fragmented siting, usually resulting in any case more from circumstances and unforeseen extensions than from deliberate policy, will necessarily foster interchange between the university and its environment.

Dispersal has in fact been used on occasion as a means of weakening the institution, by putting obstacles in the way of contacts and meetings and preventing the university from exercising a potentially dangerous critical or political function. A university scattered over numerous sites is in theory more likely to be open to its social and economic environment than the single-site university, which is more easily tempted to turn in on itself. Dispersal can draw the separate units into closer contact with the local community and make both students and academics more open to the practical realities of their environment.

But that very circumstance enhances the difficulty of identifying the university, for teachers, students and the environment alike. A university is not just an institution or a physical entity. For those who work there and for the population in general it is also a symbol of something. Lack of clear spatial identity can impair its symbolic function, which has great social importance.

Siting and architectural choices thus raise the question of the university's integration and involvement in the community around it. Neither the isolated campus nor the multi-site establishment with no co-ordination of aims, responsibilities and management foster either integration of involvement.

So we ought perhaps to look to other models, based on integrated facilities and concerted development between town/region and university. But in the present context, where new university building seems unlikely to proceed on the same scale as in earlier years, the answer does not seem to lie in architecture. A more feasible course is to try to bring about changes in status, roles and functions, in spite of spatial constraints.

2. IMAGES OF THE UNIVERSITY

As we mentioned at the start of this chapter, the difficulty of determining the significance of the university from its form of spatial development is compounded by the fact that in most OECD countries the functions ascribed to the university, or expected of it, are extremely diverse and also contradictory.

The answers to this question range from one extreme to the other. They vary from country to country, from one institution to another, sometimes from one period in the economic and political context to another, and finally they depend on the kind of person to whom the question is being put.

At the very moment when, in the United States, Kenneth Ashworth, Commissioner of Higher Education in the State of Texas, can write that "in the last twenty years American higher education systems have jeopardised our society's very future by serious decline in educational quality" [5] and the Carnegie Council on Policy Studies in Higher Education can publish a report that spares no part of the university community, an opinion poll taken in Vienna shows that Austrian citizens consider that the university is of all their institutions the one most worthy of respect [6], while a similar survey in France, run by IFOP in 1979, indicates that although the French have less confidence in university teachers than in their doctors, they still rank them well above politicians, journalists, writers and priests.

The public's view of the university is shaped by a number of factors. Without claiming to present an exhaustive list, we may distinguish at least four more or less independent factors:

— *The social position of the particular sector of opinion* being questioned, and its knowledge of university institutions.

Some sections of the population have rarely or never had anything to do with the university. The less contacts they have had with it, the more distant and prestigious the university appears to them, and the less inclined they are to excuse it for involving itself in the contradictions, conflicts and difficulties which are those of society as a whole.

People who have themselves been to university, on the other hand, have more complex and sometimes more contradictory attitudes. They identify with the university's objectives, accepting its shortcomings and difficulties, but also tend to reject the changes which may have occurred "since their time". They are more aware of the differences that may exist between the training they received and the occupational practices they apply in the working life. Yet in what may be an instinctive defence of their privileges, they often show a marked resistance to the generalisation of access to university education and qualifications, together with a concern for the maintenance of high academic standards, a concern which can only reflect well on them since such standards are presumed to have existed when they were students. They are therefore usually more critical of the way universities operate, and more concerned to preserve a number of traditional features.

26

— *What is expected of the university?*

Many surveys, in particular those carried out for CERI, indicate that the main thing individuals, especially those belonging to the least privileged groups, expect the university to provide them with is a rigorous intellectual training. This is more the expression of a desire for knowledge and personal development than a demand for vocational training. At the same time there is, especially among adult students, an insistence that their own experience should be recognised and validated, and that it should be acknowledged that the university is not the repository of truth in every field. It is the public authorities and the various groups in industry who stress the relationship between education and employment, since the university's "users" are only gradually coming to demand such a relationship under the impact of the growing crisis in the industrialised societies. Thus the OECD's Business and Industrial Advisory Committee (BIAC), representing employers' organisations, urges that the concepts of "community" and "service" should not be "interpreted in ways which may encourage higher education institutions to initiate links and promote activities with the community without careful regard to the considerable implications for public expenditure, and which might place at some risk their primary teaching and research functions, and their existing relationships with industry and business". It accordingly places particular stress on the need for higher education to be linked to "the needs of the individual and his employment", and recalls at the same time (bringing us back to the first factor) the need to preserve high academic standards: "new groups should be welcomed, but without letting the academic standard be adjusted to meet possible demands to facilitate the entry". In BIAC's view the essential mission of the university thus lies in applicable research, provision of a range of knowledge useful at enterprise level, and the production of trained graduates. On the other hand the representatives of the trade union organisations (TUAC) lay greater stress on the development of knowlege per se and the democratisation of access.

— *Differing public attitudes to particular sectors of university activity* are a third major factor contributing to the diversity of the university's image.

A clear distinction must be made here between physics, chemistry and engineering on the one hand, and the social sciences on the other.

Society is prepared to acknowledge that higher education has particular competence in the natural sciences and engineering. This it considers is a field where the university must see to it that progress is made.

Society may dispute a number of fundamental research projects, where the cost seems disproportionate in relation to the short- or medium-term applications, but it supports research workers in declaring that independence is a precondition for successful research.

The situation is not at all the same with regard to the human and social sciences. This is because these sectors have by no means achieved the same universal acceptance, because they carry a much heavier conflictual load, and, above all, because the social system is unwilling to be examined "from outside" and considers itself, not without justification, to be responsible for its own functioning. The development of the social sciences demonstrates (unlike so-called "pure science") the university's renewed interest in its immediate environment, yet the growing numbers of students in these disciplines — who it is sometimes said, in the face of statistics, will never find jobs — are viewed as a threat and as the expression of an unacceptable imperialism. The community may wish to benefit from advances in university learning, but it does not always wish to be the object of that learning or have its basic values submitted to critical examination.

In addition to these general factors governing public images of the university, there are other *more circumstantial factors*:

— The degree of development of the university system;
— The specific characteristics of university institutions;
— Variations in the images of "students" and "professors", with whom the public is always tempted to identify the university. These images are at present particularly marked by the unrest of the 1960s.

Taking the recent creation of the University of Rouen, France, as an example, three distinct phases may be observed. First, a wave of enthusiasm precedes the creation of the university: local authorities, firms, public services, associations and trade unions form discussion groups and, as with the few advanced schools and institutes already in existence, look forward to close involvement with the university. Second, when the university is being set up, it rejects any pressure from its environment: the faculty members come from all parts of France and have no *a priori* interest in the Rouen area. Their one concern is to consolidate their institution, and they have no desire to be at the beck and call of local firms or appear as backers of local politicians. The university thus shows certain reservations vis-à-vis the community. Third, barely two years after its inception, as soon as it is realised that a university involves students and academics who may raise certain problems, criticise certain elements of the community or take the lead in given activities, the community too draws back, and resists any form of institutional intrusion by the university in its decision-making bodies.

This sequence of reactions is broadly confirmed by Yves Laplume's survey of mayors of university towns in France, for the Conference of February 1980, and by the studies on the new universities in the United Kingdom or the Federal Republic of Germany.

The economic crisis, combined with the expansion of university systems, the growing numbers of students and higher research costs, and the more or less general abandonment of assumptions of indefinite progress, means that today the impact of these factors is largely negative and universities are required to render account for their use of funds and, in particular, to demonstrate their social utility. This tendency is commonest in countries where university education has become most widespread. For the United States, Norman Birnbaum has summarised the position in an article entitled Higher Education and the Federal Government [7]: "Higher education should anticipate problems and suggest solutions. The student revolt forced upon our institutions a reconsideration of traditional curricula and a re-examination of their social responsibilities; the black protest stimulated new policy towards blacks and other minorities; the ethnic consciousness led to another look at the complexity of the American heritage; and the women's movement resulted in altered institutional practices (or promises of altered practices). Our colleges and universities were surprised by these developments, just as they seem to have been caught unawares by declining growth rates and the problem of surplus younger teachers. The American people are in a critical and reflective mood, sceptical about the performance of many major institutions. Higher education cannot claim exemption from this scepticism; it draws on public goodwill, but from time to time that goodwill has to be earned anew.".

Similar trends can be found in most industrialised countries. They add to the difficulties universities already have in obtaining recognition of the role that they seek to play in an unfavourable context of the relative decline in their resources (and the increase in their expenditures) and the actual or foreseeable decline in enrolments, in the short or medium term, due to population trends.

The search for new types of students (adults, underprivileged groups), the development of new forms of activity which sometimes simply reflect the search for additional resources but can also be evidence of a genuine renewal of a university's sense of vocation — such are the reactions of a number of institutions to the crisis that they are facing, but also possibly the first signs of genuine change in the universities.

Here again, the heart of the matter in our view is the role of the university and how it is to develop.

3. THE COMMUNITY'S EXPECTATIONS AND NEEDS: TOWARDS A NEW ROLE FOR THE UNIVERSITY

Our examination of the university's image seems to reveal a very wide spectrum of attitudes, from admiration through curiosity, scepticism and indifference to outright hostility.

The most recent observations seem to indicate that many universities are coming out of their traditional posture of self-sufficiency, often for economic reasons, and endeavouring to rethink the ways in which they interact with their environment. But are such efforts meeting a corresponding demand or effective desire on the part of the community? Can closer links with its environment be merely a dream of the university? There is plenty of evidence to justify putting such a question.

"Is the Liège region really conscious of the great asset it has in its university and the contributions it could make? Does the region think as much as it should of turning to the university for help in solving its problems? Doesn't it look elsewhere and especially abroad, at higher cost, for information, research and advice which the university and the research centres it has established, or with which it is associated, could supply just as well if not better, and in a context of closer collaboration with the heads of the firm or body asking for the service in question?" Thus concludes the first number of a bulletin started in Liège, Belgium, in March 1977, to make the contribution the university can make to the region known as widely as possible.

Such ignorance or indifference is not confined to any one part of the community; it is equally true of government bodies, local authorities and heads of firms.

For instance, in March 1977 the School of Commerce and Business Management in Bordeaux, France, was asked by the monthly *Le Monde de l'Éducation* to carry out a study on the links between firms in Aquitaine and the university. The findings indicate that firms make little use of research and training facilities. Of 131 firms covered by the survey, four (3 per cent) had research contracts with the university (all four employed over 100 people). 77 per cent of the firms concerned did not know what services the university can provide. Those which had some idea mentioned continuing training (15 per cent), case studies (7 per cent), training for executives (5.3 per cent), computerised management (4.6 per cent), technical studies (4 per cent), the regional and urban economy (1.5 per cent), documentation (1.5 per cent), and translation of contracts (0.76 per cent). A third of the firms had not arranged any continuing training for their executives (45 per cent of the firms employing less than 50 people). Twenty firms out of 131 (15 per cent) looked to the university for continuing training for their senior staff.

Links and contracts, when they exist, are only with the big firms which already employ graduates and have some experience of research. On the other side of France, in Alsace, in quite a different cultural and economic context, another survey by *Le Monde*, in 1978, confirmed the findings in Bordeaux: "Our contacts with firms are generally established at national or international level and local contacts often come about by chance as, for example, when the company has an applied research laboratory in the region." These are the words of the vice-president of the research department of the University of Haute-Alsace, Mulhouse.

At the Louis-Pasteur University, Strasbourg, fundamental research and contracts with public bodies predominate, especially in chemistry, neurochemistry and nuclear physics. When efforts are made to establish links with the surrounding economy the big firms are the first to benefit, as the President of the University explains: "contact is more easily established with them through their laboratories, which talk the same language as we do, and some of whose researchers were trained by us."

However, both BIAC and governments are keen for the university to make its research and consulting facilities available to small and medium-sized firms, and also to the local authorities which lack the resources to conduct their own research.

A report by the University of Waterloo, Canada, also mentions the low level of actual demand: "Industry has been very reluctant, with possible rare exceptions, to support any long-term basic research activity. Perhaps one of the major causes of this somewhat unbalanced research pattern is the fact that the growth of secondary industry in Canada is relatively recent. This has meant that up to now industrial management has been concerned almost exclusively with the many elementary and short-range needs and opportunities for engineering work, and an appreciation of the role of longer-range considerations has consequently been slow to develop. In Canadian universities there has thus been no real counterbalance to the forces which tend to decrease the connections between university and society."

Links are hardly more satisfactory when we consider specific groups of citizens. The report by the University of California [8] considers the "special interest groups", "traditional community groups" and "low income groups", and points out in each case that they have had to give up hope of any real assistance from the university: "The needs vary widely. One group wants an analysis of the adverse environmental impact of nuclear reactors; another, a study of watershed damage from logging; a third, a projection of the educational advantages of desegregation; another, research on the damage to health from DDT in coho salmon. Often their adversaries are governmental agencies and they contend that the university is the best and most likely source of impartial research to offset the bureaucratic biases in the research funded by those adversaries. Almost always such groups lack the funds to compete with their well-financed foes.

"The university as an institution has tended not to respond to the requests of such groups, sometimes because of a reluctance to become involved in politically charged and highly controversial issues. Individual faculty members have often been responsive, but when the research work goes beyond their particular capabilities and available time, it tends not to get done. When their research goes against the views of the particular agency funding the research enterprise of which they are a part, as in the case of the AEC laboratories in the controversy over reactor safety, it becomes increasingly difficult for the individual faculty members to assist these community groups."

Lastly, it does seem that very often the university fails in its efforts to promote more justice and equality. Workers, in particular, do not speak the same language as the higher educational institutions, and while showing no hostility to them do not expect them to do much to change their status. "Many workers, while not hostile to the university, do not see such an institution as being of much personal significance to themselves." (Canadian Labour Congress) [9]. E. Bockstael's survey of American trade unionists for the OECD Conference in February 1980 came to similar conclusions.

The situation is hardly more promising when the community is defined as a cultural and regional area. The notion that the university should participate in the cultural development of the region is relatively recent. Up to now, education systems have mainly helped to promote a dominant national culture at the expense of local or minority sub-cultures. Thus, whatever desires are expressed by the universities, it would be illusory to regard them as an effective means of defending cultural heritages which may often be victims of urbanisation, a drift from the land, or the diffusion by the mass media of master models to which higher education has contributed through its development. Admittedly, projects for the development of local languages and cultures, or for the revival of threatened traditions, are to be found in all Member countries. But linguistic research, for example, is more likely to be carried out for the benefit of the language in which it is written than for the one it refers to. Accordingly, almost invariably the systems of higher education exert rather a function of national homogenisation than one of local or regional differentiation.

So whether we look at the university's links with the economy, integration with the immediate environment or its component groups, the promotion of democratisation or participation in regional policy, we find a curious mixture of specific demands and indifference, expectations and distrust.

4. THE UNIVERSITY'S PLACE IN SOCIETY: AN IRREDUCIBLE CONFLICT

The foregoing observations should not be taken as implying that the various groups and bodies in the community reject or condemn the university. Criticism, occasionally quite sharp, does not mean that the university has lost its prestige. Even when degrees prove valueless for employment purposes, access to the university is still regarded as a step upwards. Increasing numbers of people wish to follow post-secondary courses without necessarily acquiring qualifications, as these have no immediate economic value. To put it another way, the present crisis has resulted both in an accentuation of the trend towards job-oriented training in the university, and in the development of purely "cultural" functions.

Students see the university as a haven of relaxation and emancipation in which they can take refuge at an age when they are increasingly beset by parent/children conflicts, uncertainty about the future, and a desire to postpone their inevitable involvement.

For older students it provides a means of putting their day-to-day worries in perspective and taking stock. The two views of the university thus converge. All who attend a university benefit from its prestige. The student is considered to be too young to have any right to participate in social conflicts, or to have any responsibility for handling the problems of daily life, but he is entitled to play the mentor among those of his own generation. He has access to studies and sources of information which enable him to know things about the major problems which the general run of the population admit they do not know. Popular reactions to what are regarded as student excesses are often expressed with benevolence, understanding and interest, even when there is an obvious feeling of irritation. The student occupies a specific place in the community's scale of values; students are not a social class, but a valuable élite. The student is an intellectual, and opinion is often biased in his favour in any circumstance — an attitude that is, incidentally, particularly noticeable in the developing countries.

In most cases, academics and the community agree in considering the university as a thing apart.

For the academic, the university is a place specially intended for critical thought and research, the chief object being the perpetuation of its structure, the maintenance of its credibility, the conservation of its "brand image".

For the community, the university is a place specially intended for research and higher education. It is a reassuring luxury, and may be the place where some counterpoise to the ill-defined forces of authority and politics can be fashioned.

The university is thus criticised for remaining an ivory tower, yet that is in the main what it is expected to be. Society does not ask the university to grapple with the problems of the day: its first duty is to remain outside the time dimension. This privileged status is enhanced still further when it comes to problems of research. The prodigious advances made by university disciplines over the last fifty years has enabled them to hold the uninitiated spell-bound. It is easy for academics to acquire the stature of "master magicians" once they have become undisputed specialists with a special language, sometimes a mumbo-jumbo, of their own.

So on the one hand universities are said to show insufficient interest in community affairs, and in the economic and social consequences of their research and their teaching. On the other hand, there is considerable concern that the university system should not lose its way by over-direct involvement in the management of day-to-day affairs.

There is a kind of deep-rooted intellectual complicity between some academics who are concerned to protect and safeguard their independence, and some members of the community, in particular economic and political decision-makers, who refuse to allow their management activities to be critically reviewed by higher education institutions, which are held to have no competence in this sphere or to be trespassing outside their proper fields.

The frequently heard proposition that the university should involve itself more thoroughly in the business of society, and assume its social responsibilities more fully, is hence an extremely ambiguous one.

That ambiguity is clearly present in the concept of scientific objectivity and the numerous senses given to it. Sometimes the emphasis is put on the possibility or even the necessity of subjecting everything to critical review; at the other times the stress is on neutrality, understood as non-involvement, and on restricting the university's functions simply to the production and dissemination of knowledge.

5. CONCLUSION

It is important to acknowledge the multiple and sometimes contradictory images of the universities, and the necessarily contradictory demands for independence and concrete involvement — a conflict of aims between the university on the one hand and the social system on the other which has been sharpened by the crisis. To recognise this is to recognise that relations between the university and the environment are highly complex, and that there can be no miracle solution which would re-establish a consensus or mutual trust, something which has never in fact existed except among very restricted groups which are themselves products of the university world. The purpose of this report is to put forward a number of actual cases from which models can be developed for forms of interaction which, starting from accepted differences, will help to produce ways and means of overcoming them. The chapters which follow describe these possible forms of interaction, list the institutions on which they depend, and examine their consequences for the institutional working of universities and also for their educational and research functions.

It was an essential preliminary to point out that the university's status is contradictory: the social system looks to the university to preserve the utmost independence from it, and at the same time demands that it be accountable. Moreover, academics and students — and it would be difficult to blame them for it — have constantly sought to play both roles, presenting themselves as citizens concerned to exert their freedom to criticise, and as a privileged group concerned to safeguard their independence. In addition, however democratic or undemocratic its policies are, the university will be viewed in different ways according to one's social group and one's chances of entering the university and of getting something out of it. No university policy which is not at the same time a social policy can change that fact.

The purpose of this chapter was accordingly to make it clear that any definition or even description of the university is bound to describe the way that the university fits into the social fabric and the way that society perceives it. There is no essential difference between the traditional functions of teaching and research and the new social functions whose development we shall analyse. Even the traditional functions cannot be understood unless it is recognised that they too are particular kinds of interactions with the environment.

Chapter 2

SERVICES, INTERACTIONS OR INTERVENTIONS?

Examination of the ways in which society sees the university system shows the extent to which the general public perceives the university as a teaching institution. The research function is not really understood. The fact that academics can participate in the development of knowledge is attributed to their private activity, made possible by teaching schedules whose significance is not understood. It is rarely related to their statutory function. The general view of the teaching function itself has not changed very much. The development of university courses for adults, through people in work becoming part-time students or through continuing education schemes directed at new groups and not leading to the traditional qualifications, has brought little change to the university's image. Only a small proportion of the potential user population is aware that it could go to university. In any case, the difficulties of combining working career, private life and university education present an obstacle that possible candidates for degree courses find hard to overcome.

We have also seen that people with no experience of higher education — still the great majority of the population — have the impression that the university world shares very few of their hopes, aspirations and interests. At the same time, they are concerned not to allow the university system to participate directly in the conduct of affairs. For the general public, the university cannot itself become an agent of change without betraying its nature and essential aims.

At the same time, however, as a result first of university expansion and then of the economic crisis, community pressure for greater control over the operation of higher education has increased. This pressure is accompanied by the oft-heard demand for the universities to involve themselves more wholeheartedly in the economic, social and cultural problems of their environment, and has redefined the function of service and positioned it alongside the functions of teaching and research. This identification of three distinct functions — teaching, research and service — is convenient *even though service to the community, as generally understood, in fact embraces the first two*. It indicates that some kinds of interaction between the community and the university are not expressed through the traditional forms of teaching and research.

Generally speaking, relatively little importance is accorded to the service function in most countries. The concept is admittedly an ambiguous one: perhaps "action" or "interaction" with the community would be more meaningful, implying positive intervention by the higher education system in the analysis of social needs and the possible means of meeting them. "Interaction" indicates that the relationship is two-way, not simply a matter of subjecting the university to outside pressures. In what follows we keep to the term "service" simply because it is the one most commonly used.

Higher education institutions have very different views about the service function and the way it is to be performed in relation to research and teaching. That is no doubt one of the most striking differences between universities and other establishments, but whatever approach is chosen it leads sooner or later to the need for institutions, *and particularly the universities*, to define their role more effectively in the face of increasing pressure and growing demands from the community.

Before analysing the service function, however, we should like to recall that what we term "the community" is in fact a complex and sometimes conflicting entity. The possibility, or even the thought, of calling upon the university depends upon one's information about its activities, one's sense of belonging to the same social group, one's experience of the role and possibilities of research, and sometimes simply on how near one is to it. The financial aspects are also relevant. Quite a number of firms (even small ones), local authorities and associations or interest groups can afford to pay for joint projects or work commissioned from a university. But what is the position when the request comes from an institution or group without sufficient funds?

In other words, unless care is taken to devise new forms of financing, the development of service to the community, far from extending the impact of the university, may tighten still further its links with the upper classes of society and the most advanced firms, benefit urban communities rather than rural ones, and remain the preserver of culturally and economically privileged groups.

1. TWO GENERALLY ACCEPTED SENSES OF THE CONCEPT OF SERVICE

The concept of service has a relatively long history, though that does not mean that it is clear to those who use and develop it. A report by the University of California [8] has correctly noted that: "...while public service is almost always identified as one of the three purposes of the university, the nature of this component, especially with respect to research, has rarely been defined. The problem is not so much that the university denies its public service role, but that no one has really been able to define what that role is. When it has been defined, traditional forms of community service that call on none of the faculty members' professional skills are often given equal weight with applied research work of a major public nature."

Historically, the idea of university service to the community came of age with the creation of the Land Grant Colleges, in the United States (the Morrill Act of 1862). In addition to their training activity in the rural world, a second piece of legislation (the Hatch Act of 1887) gave them the resources to conduct applied research and engage in experimental work. These Colleges played a fundamental part not only in agriculture but in the industrialisation of the regions in which they were set up. They broke down — a century ago — the privileges which had been unilaterally granted to academic disciplines over the arts and technologies (itself a surprising retreat from the thinking of the 18th-century encyclopaedists). A third consequence was the diversification of the curricula offered to students, at a time when Europe was still clinging to a few extremely rigid patterns. So in practice, higher education in America considered itself even in the last century to have a triple function which enabled certain Land Grant Colleges ultimately to become some of the top-ranking American universities (University of California, Cornell, University of Wisconsin, for example).

Even so, service is defined in two quite different ways, both in the United States — where attitudes have fostered fairly close relations between the university and society — and in the other OECD countries. *Under the first definition, service covers all the university's activities and merely reflects the fact that all research or teaching is ultimately of service to the community.* Whether teachers, doctors and engineers are being trained or new knowledge is being developed, whether the education is basic or continuing, whether research is fundamental or applied, it all constitutes a service and in fact depends on the community since the latter regulates these activities by giving or withholding the necessary financial resources.

This first definition of service relates solely to the relevance of the teaching or research to the community's actual problems, in contrast to the traditional detachment of the university.

This approach is clearly expressed in a number of publications by Rutgers University in the United States [10], which takes the view that each part of the university must give serious consideration to its public service role and annually ask whether its priorities, either financial or in the identification of problems, are presently relevant and are having significant impact.

This concept of service was developed in a declaration on public service activities in 1975, placing emphasis on two dimensions: service is seen essentially as technical and scientific assistance, and it must be available to the entire population.

The key concept is the application of knowledge, and Rutgers University thus re-echoes the definition of Alfred North Whitehead: "In the process of learning there should be present, in some sense or other, a subordinate activity of application. In fact, the applications are part of the knowledge. For the very meaning of the things is wrapped up in the relationships beyond themselves. Thus, unapplied knowledge is knowledge short of its meaning."

This view of service is thus based on a whole theory of knowledge and more or less explicitly criticises the traditional forms of research. Such criticism is moreover often echoed by observers outside the university, who believe that the non-applicability of knowledge is at the root of all the university's troubles. This type of criticism was particularly prominent at the end of the 1960s [11].

Other approaches concentrate more on the teaching function, and hence give greater importance to widening the range of clients than to the application of research. A number of observations, largely from universities in the United States and Canada, are of interest here.

"While the mission of any university is primarily an educational mission, the services which it may render to communities of interest must not be defined exclusively in terms of formally structured education. Rather, it is the sense of this Committee that positive extra—university impact... be it educational, economic, psychologic, or sociologic... must be viewed as an operational definition of 'service'." (University of Western Michigan).

"The functions of this institution are teaching, research and public service (not action). Public service is here defined as a university-client relationship other than a teaching-student relationship (e.g. providing assistance in formulating a municipal code)... The function of university continuing education is to assist communities in learning solutions to problems; not to institute or become participant in action programs or advocacy. The university can be a catalyst, a resource for learning, even a convener, but not an advocate." (University of Oklahoma)

While giving first place to teaching, the University of Illinois describes various forms of service, but the essential criterion is extending the range of potential users. "Public service is the all-inclusive term and 'continuing education' is a major subset, with the latter including credit courses and non-credit instruction, such as conferences and workshops for non-resident adults who participate on a part-time or short-term basis. With this instructional component of 'continuing education' taken out, the remaining 'public service' includes applied research, demonstration, knowledge dissemination, technical assistance, consultation, and a host of non-instructional services directed to problems or to decisions by individuals or institutions, public and private."

This interpretation of the service concept is not so remote as it first seems from that current in Europe. For example, the universities of the United Kingdom have had considerable extra-mural programmes for the local non-student population for a century or more. Recently, activities of this kind have developed almost everywhere in Europe, in the form either of general cultural or preparatory occupational courses.

Canada is perhaps the country in which the "citizen-student" theme, combined with the concept of the "educational city", has become most widespread [12].

The danger, both with the applicability of knowledge and with extending the range of users, is that the environment will come to be regarded as a local testing ground for work done in the university, so that a kind of university imperialism develops under the cover of service. It may be naive or dangerous to put it as plainly as the University of Amsterdam has — yet which university can fail to recognise in the following something of its own attitude?: "…As far as possible… we use the local/regional community as our laboratory from which we get the problem and the information needed for our research and education." But the members of the community sometimes object to being reduced to specimens for use in "practical studies", as the University of Cincinnati points out. "All too often, studies are conducted in communities for the purpose of students' edification and the advancement of research solely. Community leaders in the Cincinnati area have decried this practice. As a result, in some areas, such as public education systems, joint committees of university and public school personnel have been formed to monitor research activities within the schools so that all might benefit.".

The surveys by E. Bockstael in the United States and Y. Laplume in France confirm the public's mistrust of the desire of some universities to regard their entire activity as a service, a desire which expresses both a concern to justify their activity and a kind of intellectual imperialism.

The second major sense in which service is understood, on the other hand, stresses that it is a separate function:
- it is exercised concurrently with the first two but not through them;
- it represents a more or less separate element in the institutional structure;
- its object is to respond to the specific problems of a clientele which is distinct from the university community and is responsible for formulating its own needs;
- even when service takes the form of teaching or research, then, as Cerych has put it, the teaching is different in both form and content, and the research is different at least in its immediate application [13].

The characteristics of the service function in this independent sense depend on several factors. The first is the university's concept of the community. Approaches conceived in structural terms (organisation in social groups or strata), in geographical and administrative terms (immediate environment — local authorities — regions, etc.) or in socio-political terms will each tend to foster different forms of service. The next chapter accordingly deals with the ambiguities in the concept of the community.

The second factor is the local or temporary nature of the action in question. A service may well be provided without there being any interpenetration between the community and the university. When an institute of technology supplies local firms with qualified staff it is a matter of service rather than integration. The point of impact may change with circumstances, moreover. For example, the University of Puerto Rico responded to a specifically local problem — disquieting social trends and a shortage of suitable professionals — by setting up a degree course in "the arts and social welfare".

In theory an activity of this kind ought to stop once the need has been met, or else be handed over to a specialised institution. But if the programme develops into a series of research projects, or has an impact on the general lines of teaching in sociology, economics or psychology, then it becomes a matter of interaction rather than of service alone.

A third factor — really an extension of the previous one — is whether the service is direct or indirect. The following passage, in which the University of New England,

Australia, presents a new programme, is particularly explicit on this point: "The effects on teaching and research will be indirect, but the effects on action (e.g. service) will hopefully be direct and significant. The intention is that the project influence the way the community (i.e. the nation and its component sectors) regards and manages its rural sector."

This concept of service is particularly interesting since it is the one which generates the greatest resistance, both on account of the view of teaching and research that underpins it and because it is liable to put the university in a contradictory position, caught between multiple demands that no internal policy can rank in order of importance.

The fact that a service — be it scientific or social, for industry or for the region as a whole — is practical and immediate can well be misleading, since by definition one service excludes another, either because needs are numerous and occasionally contradictory or because of the inevitable limits on human and material resources.

A joint paper by the University of Massachusetts and the State University of New York stresses the danger of contradictions: "Universities have, in a sense, created the uncomfortable position in which they now find themselves through unwittingly imprecise semantics. Universities do not provide direct social services and a strong case can be made why to do so would be inappropriate. There is something inconsistent about becoming too involved with client relationships while trying to think objectively about problems and solutions inherent in a particular situation, or while conceptualising relationship as part of the educational process." [14].

Universities ought not become "service stations" (to use Asa Briggs' expression), pulled in contrary directions by their environment and incapable of furnishing anything more than a superficial assessment of any situation.

Adoption of the service concept thus involves considerable dangers that various universities may lose their real significance. Rather than listing cases exhaustively, it seems appropriate to seek to identify what we shall term the levels of the university's intervention and to compare the consequences of its intervention with some of the essential characteristics of the university.

2. FORMS OF UNIVERSITY SERVICE AND LEVELS OF INTERVENTION

The preliminary surveys for the 1980 Conference and the discussions at the Conference itself provided a large number of suggested classifications, some based on the nature of services, some on the degree of institutionalisation (from an individual service to a redefinition of the general policy of the university), and some on the different kinds of services provided, this last order of classification sub-dividing into two, depending on whether the university puts its existing facilities or current production at the disposal of the community, or whether it responds to specific requests for services such as teaching, research, consulting, monitoring and supervision or *co-operation*, the latter being seen as assistance in decision-making (problem analysis) or assistance in implementation.

Rutgers University suggests four major categories of services, distinguishing between individual and institutional services in each case.

— Technical assistance, advice and information provided directly to government, public and community groups in areas where the university has appropriate expertise. Examples: a school of business initiates a programme to promote entrepreneurship and professional management among minorities

39

(institutional activity); a professor provides testimony on an environmental protection bill to the state legislature (individual activity).
— Research towards the solution of public policy problems conducted by members of the faculty and staff, alone or in groups. Examples: a school of law accepts responsibility to codify a body of law or to help modernise a state court system; a professor serves on a governor's tax policy commission.
— Conferences, seminars, workshops, short courses and other non-degree-oriented upgrading and training for government officials, social service personnel, professional people, business executives, and citizens. Examples: Cook College provides a series of state-wide seminars on methods of land-use planning; a professor assists a state agency on a conference or seminar in his speciality.
— Administrative as well as substantive support when some element of the public looks to the university for financial support or an organisational structure within which a programme or service may operate.

But the Rutgers contribution then brings in a factor which goes beyond this classification and leads on to the question of the way in which the university may intervene.

"The public service activity of the university should involve problem identification as well as problem solving. The university has an obligation to analyse a question or issue and to suggest alternatives heretofore unrecognised. In short, the public service responsibility of a university should include the raising of questions and alternatives not foreseen in the original request."

"Public service at Rutgers should go beyond the response to specific requests to take initiative in seeking out new ways in which resources can be applied to the needs of the people of the state."

Using this approach, we propose to consider some of the different ways in which service can be provided, including what may be called the "levels of intervention" at which they occur, and which may have fundamentally different implications. Five different ways of providing service can be distinguished:
— The university puts its facilities and human resources at the disposal of the community and disseminates its traditional products (graduates, new knowledge).
— Execution of "orders" placed by the community.
— Analysis of needs.
— Analysis of problems at the request of the community.
— The university implements a particular solution where this is compatible with its institutional status.

a) The university puts its equipment, infrastructure and human resources at the disposal of the community:
— Use of equipment, premises, laboratories, etc; the university may open its library to the public, make its publications available, provide premises for lectures and meetings, or allow outside use of its laboratories, industrial plant, television facilities, and data processing systems, as well as its sports and cultural facilities. By definition, the closer such users are to the university, the more use they can make of it;
— Use of teachers and students: it is worth noting that students can make a considerable contribution to community development, and derive great benefit from it for their own personal development (cf. the "study-service" system particularly common in the United States and the United Kingdom, and of which we shall have more to say in Part Two, Chapter 1). Nearness to the university is not so important in this case.

40

- Conversely, for there to be a proper response to the needs for occupational training, education and research the community must put its equipment, infrastructural and human resources (e.g. people in industry and business acting as teachers) at the disposal of the higher education institution. An inventory of what each side can supply would seem to be a prerequisite for co-ordinating activities of this kind.

Lifelong education and opening up all courses to a widening population may be considered as a further means of disseminating the university's activities and making them available to the community.

This first procedure for the provision of service thus includes making the university's own "product" (i.e. teaching, research, information it possesses) available to the environment.

The main difficulty here, as we have already pointed out, is the weakness of information flows. The stress placed on this question was perhaps the most significant contribution by the Federal German and Austrian University Rectors Conferences and the Finnish representatives to the OECD 1980 Conference, but it is surprising to note that American universities, the ones most committed to the service function, also deplore the very low level of information exchanges. The University of California, for instance, noted that "for an effective transfer of the results of research from producer to consumer much more is required than simply supplying data published in technical journals or on a set of computer tapes. Legislators, control officials, the media and public need research results put into a form that they can understand, assimilate and use directly in the solution of their problems. This requires alternative forms of communication, different channels, and different techniques for reaching various publics...", and the State University of New York at Albany [15] observed that " the contributions of this university to the region and the state have not been adequately publicised. Even those programmes which make an obvious contribution, and have an important impact on people in this region have not been clearly and adequately presented to the public. It's as if we were saying:'Everyone knows we're great, so why tell them about it'. That stance may have been satisfactory before this was a university centre, and when Albany State indeed did have widespread recognition as a teacher's college. Such a position is clearly not appropriate today, and more effective means of publicising the university's contribution need to be found."

In conclusion, the main feature of this first form of service provision seems to be that it involves communication and exchange rather than interaction properly so-called, and there is no question of a new function or even of a change in the normal functioning of the universities. What we have in fact described are the circumstances in which the university's traditional activities may be regarded as to some extent a public service.

b) *The second form of service provision by the university is the execution of "orders" placed by the community.* The order may be for training, whether occupational or in continuing education, it may be for a cultural activity. It may also be for fundamental or applied research.

In most cases the "order" is entirely defined by the "customer". It is the customer who decides what his need is and such solution suits him. The university is called in because it is considered competent, and specific arrangements for payment are agreed between the two sides.

The bulk of the concrete cases we have analysed fall into this category. Such arrangements are particularly widespread in the United States, but lifelong training activities, research contracts and other services are also negotiated on these lines in France and Belgium. The customer may apply to a member of the institution, negotiating with him and engaging his services for a given period, or deal directly with

41

the university, which subcontracts the service to a department or to one or more individuals.

This is undoubtedly the form that can best be described as a service, for a number of reasons:

- *The function concerned is definitely not university teaching or research* even if the service ultimately involves some research or teaching (hence the expression "third dimension");
- *It is this type of intervention that raises fears of the university turning into a "service station".* The activities involved are in fact fragmented, local and prompted by a current problem. The university is in competition with other suppliers of services and therefore adheres as closely as possible to the order it receives, selling its intellectual autonomy for a little financial autonomy;
- *In this type of service it is the customer who calls the tune.* Strictly speaking it is not a new form of co-operation between environment and higher education, since it is the environment which decides the profile and number of the people who are to be trained, or the form the research is to take. The university's say is confined to the way the order is carried out.
- To conclude, this kind of service does not change the university, which carries on its teaching and research as before, without any disruption. Any fallout there may be for the university's structure or teaching methods (see Part Three, Chapters 1 and 2) has no impact on service. *All that is required from the university is that it should be competent, available, efficient and less expensive than other competent organisations.*

c)   *Participation in the analysis of the community's needs, the third form of service provision*, may be based on an order placed by the community. The order is generally instigated by the university, which considers such participation essential if some part of its teaching and research programmes is to be constantly adjusted to the needs of the local, regional or national community.

Apart from the question of initiative, which as we have seen may be shared, this form of intervention differs sharply from the previous levels in at least two ways.

- We saw earlier that a "service" is a response to an order placed and defined by the community. The community's definition of the order generally does no more than reproduce a model borrowed from elsewhere in society or from theoretical profiles devised by universities. That is why, for this third level, we prefer the term "action" as defined earlier, because a different conception of the university's role is involved here. It presupposes that the community accepts that the university can conduct research and suggest solutions without reference to any prior options by the community, and it also presupposes that the university is acknowledged as a legitimate critical authority. None of this can come about without conflict. At this level a number of obstacles to the development of relations with the immediate environment emerge. In actual fact, the contradictions or problems which arise are due to an inadequate definition of the links between the university and the environment and the type of services the university is asked to supply. A contradiction arises between its international, national and regional vocations, for instance, when the university overemphasizes occupational training designed to fit students for existing jobs or improvises replies to questions which are formulated outside the university and independently of it. On the other hand, a university capable of analysing practical problems and defining relevant research and training profiles may become a more efficient structure for national or international activities.
  A university may thus feel free to criticise the order it has received, redefine

the needs, or suggest a solution not hitherto envisaged. An example from France was the training proposed by the Université des Sciences Sociales, Grenoble, when nearby councils asked for help with local government tasks. The result was the establishment of a training centre for local authority staff on lines quite different from those envisaged by the initiators[16]. There are numerous examples of such shifts in emphasis, and of the negative reactions that they sometimes produce.

— The other difference lies in these actions' impact on university structure. In other words, the ability to participate in the analysis of problems and hence in the definition of demand presupposes that the university is prepared to make a number of adjustments:

— The establishment of horizontal or transversal structures combining different disciplines and departments;

— Changes in some research programmes to adapt them to practical situations;

— Changes in the university's teaching methods, and even in the definitions of the profile and training of its academic staff;

— A change in the university's language and the abandonment of any demand that the public should adopt its jargon in order to benefit from its knowledge. Strange though it may seem, experience has shown that no such changes are needed for the categories of service provision described earlier. When the community calls in academics it knows what to expect. But when a university claims to anticipate social demand it must shed its academic language, however legitimate it may be scientifically.

Adelaide University, Australia[17], urged that " the disciplines and institutions of higher learning themselves [should overcome] their need to hide behind or protect themselves with jargon, perhaps by simply coming to terms with the community and their own context".

At this third level, what the university is being asked for is a new flexibility, a continuing capacity for change together with a new-found intellectual modesty, rather than a mere extension of its traditional activities.

d)   *A fourth way of providing service is for the university to participate, at the community's request, in analysing problems and putting forward various possible solutions.* Common examples are town planning, transport, public administration or health, all areas in which the community has decisions to take. But the community's requests are generally fragmented and sometimes inconsistent, and may well lead scientific thought and teaching astray by imposing dubious imperatives on them.

The concept of "need" to which requests refer is usually obscure. It is always mediated and refracted by dominant models, and has to be interpreted. What is actually expressed is not necessarily a need; it may simply be an interest.

One of the university's roles, precisely, is to preserve some protected areas of intellectual freedom where it is shielded from influences which might distort its mission. In certain cases this freedom may entail proposing new alternatives or a radical criticism of the options chosen.

To be useful, the university must be capable of looking at society and suggesting other ways for it to function. *Autonomy, and, in a certain sense, "authority" are essential if the university is to provide service of the quality expected of it.*

The point we have just made is a major one and clearly reflects the problems involved in the social and political function of the university. This emphasis on the importance of the university being able to take a detached view is quite different from the concept of a university totally impervious to the pressures exerted on it, even though in both cases the key word is "autonomy".

This may explain the disappointing results of some efforts at university/community integration. To be of use to the community, the university must not be too dependent on it. The change in the conception of the university in the socialist countries is a good illustration of this point. Some of these countries have abandoned the view that the university system must be totally subordinated to the objectives of the community, not because the primacy of community objectives has been brought "into question" but because the university cannot serve its environment unless it makes full use of its critical capacity, its autonomy of development, and its ability to make scientific analyses of the social system surrounding it.

e) Last, the university may participate in implementing a given solution, provided this is compatible with its status. There are many examples of this kind of practical commitment. The commonest and most obvious one is the work done by university hospital departments, in some cases extending to prevention, the dispensing of primary health care and health education.

This form of action, too varied to be studied here, entails co-operation with other institutions, awareness of the university's limitations, and a recognition that those strong in theory are not always the ones best able to deal with the minutiae of practical applications.

CONCLUSION

With regard to the five levels we have described the dividing line certainly lies between levels *b)* and *c)*. As soon as the possibility of the university playing a role in analysing its environment's needs is envisaged, the need for a *redefinition of the missions of the university* has to be admitted.

Such a redefinition has numerous consequences. The analysis of problems and needs, and the application of a critical approach are global procedures which are almost always interdisciplinary. They involve the university as a whole, and require in return radical changes in the university and its staff and in the traditional conception of teaching and reseach. They also presuppose that the university is independent, and accepted by its environment as a centre of initiative. New structures for participation at the level of the administration of the university system and its decision-making bodies must also be set up.

The fundamental point is that the redefinition of the university's role — critical and effective involvement with the problems of its environment, the establishment of joint institutions and two-way participation — raises a further problem which is central to all relations beween the university and the community, i.e. *how to combine commitment with neutrality, scientific objectivity with involvement in social problems and hence in social conflicts, and, in the final analysis, independence with participation.*

These points will all be discussed below, but first we need to examine a number of difficulties which are particularly bound up with analysis of the concept of service. There are four major problems.

The *first*, on which this chapter has already touched, is the obscurity of the concept of need. What is a need? Who can legitimately express it? What does responding to a need, satisfying or changing it, entail? When we speak of fuller adaptation to the needs of society we run the risk of falling into verbalism and ideological forms of thought, whereas scientific thinking originates in the adoption of a critical attitude towards such submission to accepted opinion.

The *second* problem, which follows on from the first, has to do with the concept of "relevance"; this needs to be carefully examined, especially when applied to education.

To suggest enlarging the service function of the university does not mean accepting the almost traditional criticism of university teaching (that it is cut off from everyday life and practice, archaic, unsuited to the demands of industry) generally invoked to account for the poverty of exchanges between the university system and the economic system. As Luc Boltanski[18] points out, to accept this explanation means closing one's eyes to a number of well-known facts.

— The work graduates actually do is relatively independent of what they have been formally trained to do. Whether they are awarded by specialist institutions or universities (and excluding medicine and certain forms of engineering), the technical qualifications acquired are not decisive in determining subsequent careers. Surveys conducted by the French monthly *"Expansion"*, for instance, show that 46 per cent of data-processing specialists have degrees in arts, law or political science, or have had no formal higher education. Among business executives, only 24 per cent are graduates of business schools, 19 per cent engineering graduates and 13 per cent university or political science graduates, while 44 per cent have had no formal higher education.

— The mobility of executive grades, which increased dramatically in the period 1960 to 1975, largely at the behest of employers, widens the gap between formal academic qualifications and the functions actually performed.

— Continuing education accentuates the lack of relationship between the level and nature of the job held and the characteristics of the incumbent's initial training.

So it is not a matter of proposing fuller "adaptation" by the university. Adaptability would seem to be far better ensured by providing a high level of general education than by short-lived technical qualifications. It is more a matter of shifting the balance of the tasks entrusted to the university. What is "relevant" for both the individual and society may be a set of general skills, precisely the skills which form the basis of the ability to analyse problems and to suggest alternatives, rather than training which enables one faithfully to carry out orders[19].

A *third* question concerns the differences between the model underlying the functioning of the university and the model underlying the functioning of society as a whole, including other research or higher education institutions. Promoting a change in the university's missions, advocating more interactions between university and community and considering that this will generate a positive dynamic, does not mean subjecting one model to the other; it means making full use of what is original — deviant in some people's view — in the university model. That is why we have laid stress on the level of intervention, rather than on the content of service, and have particularly recommended levels *c*) and *d*). This approach can hardly be better justified than by quoting at length from a paper presented by Manfried Welan, Rector of the Vienna Agricultural University (Austria), at the seminar on "Strategies for developing the public image of institutions of higher education" organised by CERI/IMHE in September 1981 in Munich.

"Considering all the difficulties and the structural properties of the universities one may wonder why they still exist. Both their organisation and their goals make the universities deviant phenomena. Universities can rightfully be called the nonconformists among institutions. By combining research and teaching in a framework of relative independence, they differ sharply from the other agencies of knowledge production and transmission, like the research institutes, the schools which teach practical skills, or the mass media which market knowledge for consumption. In contrast to

45

universities, these agencies are more or less strictly controlled by plan, market, or political priorities. Universities are relatively independent from the exchange principle, from supply and demand, from economic and political competition, from elections, majorities and opinions. They are not acting under the pressure of short-term assignments. They have more and a different time than the institutions of the political-economic-administrative system. They experience neither a great fluctuation in goals nor excessive pressures towards adaptation. Their tasks, research and teaching, are laid down in a highly general fashion. By virtue of this stability and continuity and by their independence from short-term decisions of other systems the universities are a veritable anomaly in an economized and administered world. The separation of work and leisure plays a much smaller role than elsewhere: individual independence is greater than in any other setting. Amidst the "realm of necessity", the contours of a "realm of freedom" are visible, in which work is expended as a creative activity. But precisely the relative freedom and independence of university members makes them and their institution a favourite target for the attacks of other, less privileged groups. Yet, in spite of all attempts to create institutional uniformity, the university has hitherto weathered the storms and been able to retain its previous position. This longevity is mainly due to the above-mentioned cultural functions of the universities. The basic value pattern of industrial society is grouped around the belief in "rational action" in every field of life. Science is the ultimate arbiter of what constitues rationality, and because of the principle of internal consistency it is its sole arbiter in its own field of scientific questions. Each single function of the university could be performed more efficiently by specialised research or teaching institutions. But the uniqueness of the university lies in its combination of functions, which makes it a symbol of rational authority. Maybe this symbolic value gives the universities the strength to defy encroachment on their traditional rights."

Last, the *fourth* problem involves a paradox which is perhaps what the universities are liable to resist most strongly. For most university research workers and academics, their environment consists largely of their peers, the international community of learning. Yet when we look closely at the various forms the provision of service we have described can take, it may be assumed that the "richer" the form of provision — "rich" here meaning at one and the same time complex, allowing a large measure of freedom to suggest solutions, involving a multi-referential approach, and bringing various parts of the community and the university into play — the more the "radius of action" of the "service" envisaged is liable to be confined to a given environment. Developing interactions with that environment hence entails a fresh review of the meaning of the university's universality, and of the importance of "localisation". Further on we shall discuss the reasons why we attach particular significance to the concept of region (without limiting ourselves to the administrative definitions of individual Member countries), but it does seem that a review of the notion of the universality of given knowledge or know-how, and specifically a somewhat more sophisticated analysis of what (depending on national and local circumstances, but also on political, cultural and social options) is meant by the *community* is in fact one of the keys to defining a university policy the consequences of which and conditions for which we are here endeavouring to identify.

Chapter 3

THE AMBIGUITIES OF THE CONCEPT OF COMMUNITY

The need to tighten up, structure and more generally develop relations between the university and its environment is quite commonly recognised both by academics and by the national or local public authorities and the population in general. But it is based on extremely varied if not contradictory geopolitical and institutional understandings of that environment. Substituting the term "community" for "environment" only underlines the ambiguities as to the nature of that environment and more especially its heterogeneous character.

It would seem impossible in any case to limit oneself to the notion of an organised, institutionalised "community". However obvious that approach might seem, with its emphasis on administrative criteria corresponding in most cases with territorial delimitations, it seems equally obvious that it cannot be used to circumscribe the totality of interests and individuals actively concerned in relationships with the university. It would be the same if, at the other extreme, the word "community" was used to refer to the whole of the recruitment area of a particular university. Going further, if only to underline the complex and heterogeneous character of the concept, it should be noted that the "population" interested in and concerned by the university is itself in no way homogeneous, either as regards the demands which emanate from it or the channels through which these are expressed. Thus it is not surprising that, when asked in our survey for their own definition of the concept of "community", the universities referred to such different and complementary, precise and vague criteria as:

— Organised population groups/coexistence in a given geographical area;
— A certain degree of socio-economic integration/the sense of belonging to a community;
— All potential or real client-individuals/the student recruitment area/the area over which the "products" of the university are disseminated (for example, graduates, research);
and so on.

Whatever the definition chosen — and we shall see that each of them has its own limitations and ambiguities — we can agree straight away to note the existence of factors of differentiation within any "community", such as:

— Ethnic groups;
— Cultures and sub-cultures;
— Rural or urban society;
— Different degrees of socio-economic development;
— Differing structures of representation, authority, powers and responsibilities.

These factors of differentiation are important since they can lead to the exclusion of certain groups in the community from any relationship with the university, either

47

because of their ethnic group, their particular sub-culture, their inability to find channels for expressing their requests or demands, or because of their cultural, economic or spatial "distance" from the university world.

While attempts to combine or reconcile the criteria chosen by the universities and the factors of differentiation internal to the "community" can give rise to a multitude of possible definitions of the concept of "community", it is nevertheless possible, at the risk of a massive and arbitrary simplification, to identify three broad approaches to the concept of environment of the university:

- A *structural approach* based on an indentification, usually empirical, of groups of real or potential clients for higher education;
- A *geographical, institutional and administrative approach* based on more or less rigorous and detailed territorial delimitations;
- A *voluntarist approach* centred mainly on the identification of target populations and/or specific territories selected for improvement, the university being one of the chief agents of that improvement as part of its active involvement in development.

1. A "STRUCTURAL" APPROACH

The essential criterion underlying this approach is that of a real or potential client-population served by the university, which at the same time constitutes an important agent in the process of expressing and identifying social demands. With this approach it is clear that reciprocal university-community relations concern a much larger population than students in the traditional sense of the term. The operational limits of this approach remain to be defined.

Our survey in fact showed that a large number of higher education establishments use this approach, but differ considerably in their interpretation of the concept of " community" thus defined:

- There are first the universities which understand by "community" *all potential or real client-individuals*. While this definition may be somewhat vague, examination of replies to the survey for example by the University of Illinois (United States), Tampere (Finland), Ryokoku (Japan), and also most of the replies coming from the institutions of higher education in the United Kingdom, shows that the *clientèle* in question coincides in the main with the groups catered for by the permanent education and continuing training services. The areas concerned are usually social or, more broadly, socio-educational in character. The objectives aimed at are usually the updating and adjustment of new theoretical and practical knowledge and in many cases bringing levels of knowledge up to a certain standard, especially in the case of individuals whose initial level of knowledge is extremely low.
- Second, there are the universities which, under the concept of "community", emphasize the idea of a *"community of interests"*, that is to say an entity composed of formal or informal groups as the case may be. Whereas in the previous case the emphasis was on *individuals* — and therefore, on individual demands — the emphasis under this second interpretation is on *organised groups*, and especially trade union organisations as far as worker education is concerned. This kind of approach is brought out in the replies from a large number of American universities like the University of Maine at Orono, the

State University of Michigan, or the "College of Lifelong Learning" of the State University of Wayne, and the Swedish universities whose relations with trade union organisations are extremely close. It is also brought out in the analysis of the various American, French, English or Japanese experiences of direct negotiations with the trade union organisations in the ILO paper on "The role of the universities in worker education" [20]. The fact however that the groups in question may be informal, that is to say outside the normal (and normative) structures of representation, opens up a much wider perspective for the development of reciprocal university-community relations. We are thinking here of the whole of the associations' movement, and in particular of the associations for the defence of the environment and for socio-cultural activities which, by developing relations with the university, both improve the level of their arguments and reinforce their social legitimacy.

— A third connotation of the word "community" — and probably the one most often met with in current usage — is *"firms" or "employers"*. In this case university/community relations are thought of as developing along the two lines of employment-oriented education (and the continuing training of executives) and applied research for the benefit of firms. While this orientation is obvious and natural in the case of higher education establishments coming directly within the recruiting areas of firms — as is the case in France for all schools of commerce and management, but also for certain technological institutes — it is equally so for the majority of occupation-oriented institutions like, for example, the Instituts universitaires de technologie in France or the Polytechnics in the United Kingdom. The same applies to institutions such as the Technical University of Lisbon (Portugal), the Emily MacPherson College in Melbourne (Australia), the Hochschule für Verwaltungswissenschaften (College for the Sciences of Administration) of Speyer (Germany).

— Finally, yet another connotation of the term "community" identifies it more or less with the *"public authorities"*, this latter term being used to cover geopolitical entities, that is to say territorial and administrative bodies. This interpretation is more frequently found in countries like France, where the network of university establishments corresponds fairly closely to the organisation of the administrations. It is to be found also in other Member countries, for example in Norway in the case of two interdisciplinary projects run by the University of Trondheim, the one on ecology and regional planning, the other on the administration of education. To a lesser degree, the same interpretation underlies certain "components" of the University of Quebec (Chicoutimi) and the University of Acadia (Province of Nova Scotia) in Canada. Incidentally, this interpretation very often also covers the notions of "community of interest" and of "geographically defined region".

This very approximate classification of the different meanings given to the term "community" requires two further observations. Firstly, the meanings can vary depending on the discipline or faculty concerned. The Universities of Lisbon and Porto in Portugal both pointed out that, while for the Economics Faculty the "community" obviously meant "firms", for the Arts Faculty it referred rather to individuals or "communities of interest", and for the Law Faculty, which is less sensitive to the external environment, the "community" meant simply the teachers and students themselves. Secondly, these different interpretations may be combined or juxtaposed, as for example in certain modes of organisation of continuing training for adults, in which individuals, trade union groups, firms, and the public authorities are all involved in working out arrangements.

2. A GEOGRAPHICAL, INSTITUTIONAL AND ADMINISTRATIVE APPROACH

However straightforward it may seem, the criterion underlying this approach — that is to say using a territorial division to show the limits of each type of " community" — can be quite inappropriate, and even ambiguous. While it is true at first sight that one can identify territorial and functional divisions corresponding grosso modo to recruitment areas (thus the recruitment area for a primary school corresponds to a rural commune or urban district; that for a secondary school to a rural or urban administrative district, and finally those for a university and a more specialised centre for research to a region and a group of regions respectively), problems of relationships between the university and its environment transcend any conceivable type of administrative or geographical framework.

It would indeed be too simplistic and arbitrary to assign precise and definite frontiers to what one might call "a university's region" without at the same time taking into account the different functions of universities. As the Finnish submission rightly points out: "...(the university's region)... comprises the university town, the relative area of influence of the university (geographically wider than the town), its absolute areas of influence, and finally the area or areas from which its students are recruited".

To demonstrate more precisely the possible variations in the definition of a university's "environment", the following areas may be distinguished: the student recruitment area (corresponding to the *teaching* function), the area of dissemination of research activities (corresponding to the *research* function) and finally, the area over which services are provided (corresponding to the *service* function). Though they overlap the one with the other, these different areas present wide variations from one university to the other. What similarity is there indeed between a famous university which can attract students and well-known specialists from all over the national territory, which disseminates its research activities fairly widely over the whole of the national and international community, and which provides a multiplicity of services extending far beyond the interests and demands of the local environment, and a small university whose audience is (still) limited to its regional environment?

No matter how small it may be, no university seems willing to accept being enclosed in a narrowly defined area which the fact of the mobility of people (teachers, students, graduates) would at once invalidate. That is why universities seem to want to assign to themselves an area, whether in regard to the particular individuals who come to it to find the right conditions for their development, or in regard to the international scientific community, which transcends as much as possible their national and above all their local particularity. This it seems to us is the reason why, while the universities are all only too willing to recognise their functions of educating individuals and producing knowledge, functions which fit in well with this at one and the same time individual and universal view of themselves, they resist the "service" functions which enclose them in a *concrete* and therefore finite environment. They are very willing to address themselves to new sections of the population to the extent that this means an extension of their activities, but they are afraid of doing so to the extent that it means accepting narrowly defined geographical limits to those activities.

In any case to identify the "community" with the "region" makes little sense if, parallel with that, not account is taken of the fact that the term "region" itself covers territorial and political divisions which vary widely from one Member country to another [21]. It is true that the nine Austrian Länder, the fifty Spanish provinces, the twenty Italian regions, the six Japanese districts or the twenty-two French "régions de programme" are all based on politico-administrative divisions which themselves correspond more or less to physical, socio-economic and demographic entities. It by no means follows, however, that the relationships between the universities within those countries and their respective regions are all of the same nature. Any similarities are all the more unlikely in that the relationship between the regions and the central authorities varies from one country to the other.

Furthermore, starting with these same regions, further breakdowns can be made into areas corresponding either to sub-groupings or regroupings of different administrative units — like for example the Tennessee area in the United States or the Alpine area in France or Italy. It must also be remembered that certain problems may transcend national frontiers and thus concern a number of universities in different countries: obvious examples here are the studies of pollution of the Baltic Sea, those concerning the regulation of the Danube or Rhine rivers, and, on a still wider scale, the projects being undertaken in the framework of the Mediterranean Basin.

Finally it must be pointed out that in the majority of Member countries the regional question has become a major political issue, especially since, in addition to the factors connected with economic development, we are witnessing the emergence of a regional sensitivity related to the more or less recognised and confirmed existence of ethnic or linguistic minorities. This means that as far as its reciprocal relationships with the university are concerned, the region is acquiring an additional dimension which cannot fail to exert an influence on the role that the university can play and, a fortiori, on the demands which are addressed to it.

It is in a context such as this, and with all due allowance for the differences in this respect between one Member country and another (and a fortiori one region and another), that the identification of an environment with a territorial community acquires its full significance. Whether it is in fact the result of an administrative and budgetary deconcentration decided on by the central authorities with reference to the global objectives of socio-economic development and regional planning, or the result, on an more internal level within the regions themselves, of a process of socio-cultural integration and tightening up of community links, this second approach seems to have three objectives:

- On the one hand to take into account the existing disparities between regions or areas in order to ensure a better distribution of financial, human and technical resources, whilst endeavouring to introduce more equitable conditions for access to the educational services;
- On the other hand, to bring about a better adaptation of teaching and research activities to the socio-economic and cultural realities of the "regional" environment;
- And finally, to make changes, sometimes quite far-reaching, in the structures and decision-making procedures, both in the community and the university, through an increased participation of each in the other's affairs.

The relative importance of these three objectives seems moreover to depend very much on the administrative level at which the decision to adopt this approach is taken. In the case of a *geographical division of tasks* decided on by a central planning authority on the basis of global objectives laid down by a central government, this will usually mean administrative deconcentration and a redistribution between the regions of budget appropriations for education with a view to ensuring more equal access to education. For the universities working under this kind of arrangement, the emergence of closer relations with the community does not involve any significant institutional changes, and certainly no structural or teaching changes.

When, however, it is a question of *"internal" regional strategies*, worked out at the level of the local institutions, authorities or populations, and not related to any overall national policy, the experiences we have examined seem to show a tightening up of community links on the one hand, but also more radical changes in university and teaching structures. Regionalisation (or, more generally, the fixing of a well-defined territorial area) seems in fact to stimulate integration of the measures taken in various social sectors, a better allocation of community, university or private resources, and adjustment of the educational system's supply to the economic, cultural or social demands of the environment. But it requires in return an ability by the university to make a coherent response, that is to say the breaking down of the barriers between certain disciplines, more flexible teaching practices, and different ways of participating in the life of the community.

In other words it seems that the first approach is governed by a strategy centred on national or regional planning, while the second approach is governed by a more "participative" strategy the main purpose of which is to shift and transform decision-making structures and which depends on open mechanisms of regulation and negotiation.

The paradox revealed by the survey we carried out, the results of which have been confirmed by the survey made by Jean Jadot for the CERI Programme on Institutional Management in Higher Education, is that the questions of regional development, decentralisation, the necessary adjustment to local realities, receive much more prominence in the more centralised countries such as France, Finland, Portugal, Sweden or Norway, whereas the universities of federal or strongly decentralised countries seem to prefer the first type of definition of the community, which we have called the "structural" type. This observation brings us back to the assumption that in most OECD countries any suggestion of strengthening the links between the community and the university, being something new, is regarded as highly controversial by the existing structures. This controversial, and therefore dynamic, aspect of the majority of the experiments made is a major factor, irrespective of the depth and extent of those experiments. This enhances the interest of the third approach, the "voluntarist" approach, in which this innovative and transformatry function is explicitly accepted. It also tells us something about the scale of the changes it is desired to bring about. Already, in regard to "voluntary decentralisation", the OECD examiners of education policy in Norway pointed out: "undoubtedly, the only source of decentralisation decisions carrying adequate authority to have them accepted is the central government. This leaves us with the paradoxical question whether decentralisation which is initiated by central authority does not defeat itself. How can a strongly centralised system transform itself into its opposite? Is centralisation a trend which can be reversed? Or can central authority only be relinquished if it is seized, not given away (usually a process more painful than central authorities are willing to endure)?"

The same could be said of the French decision to make the universities more autonomous, a decision that was followed by the introduction of norms and rules rendered necessary by that autonomy. We could also quote other examples.

3. A "VOLUNTARIST" AND POLITICAL APPROACH

The first two approaches described above correspond very approximately to what are called "natural" social or geo-social realities. The third approach, the main thrust of which is planning aimed at defining and circumscribing "ex-ante" the community which the university is to serve, is quite different.

This approach, which is found at its most explicit when new universities are being set up, leans heavily on the contribution that these institutions can make to regional economic and industrial development (as for example in the case of the University of Luleå in Sweden or Limerick in Ireland). In doing this, the university participates in the awakening of regional awareness, especially when some of its activities (teaching, research and services) are directed towards target populations or specific geographical areas which it is intended either to improve or to assist in their own efforts at improvement. In the context of our studies, the replies submitted by universities such as that of Twente in the Netherlands, Rouen in France, the Manchester Polytechnic (United Kingdom) or Luleå, show that, in a deliberate and planned way, these institutions intend to intervene in a regional dynamic which is both social and economic, especially when the social groups or geographical areas concerned are disadvantaged ones.

More precisely, the specific objectives underlying the setting up of a "regional" university, however varied they may be in the light of the socio-economic conditions prevailing in the university's environment, aim on the whole at developing an intellectual infrastructure capable of contributing to the development of the region which hitherto had been considered as (relatively) disadvantaged. The objectives are:

- To develop in the region a general climate favouring research;
- To give a fresh impetus to firms and to other local activities;
- To offer a wider variety of programmes, both for university studies and for occupational training;
- To improve the supply, on the labour market, of university graduates capable of filling responsible posts.

There is therefore an obvious link between voluntarist policies and an "instrumental" conception of higher education, this being understood as capable of deliberately bringing about a number of economic, cultural and social effects envisaged in their globality.

CONCLUSION

After the brief presentation given above, it should not be thought that the three approaches to the concept of "community" we have described are based on homogeneous classification principles. It is in fact not possible to give precise meanings to the terms "environment" and "region", and while it is obvious that the field of action of a university will vary according to its functions and its activities, it is also essential to recognise that the demands made on the university by its environment will vary considerably in significance and weight.

If we have nevertheless emphasized the importance of defining the understandings which the actors involved in these relationships have of the community, then that is because those understandings largely determine the type of strategy which will be adopted to develop those relationships.

We must also be careful not to neglect the fact that those relationships and the strategies for developing them are part of a dynamic, by its nature conflictual and continuing, in the context of which the concept of "community" can be made to change, or to take on different and sometimes conflicting acceptations.

An examination of the actual ways in which the universities use the relationships they have with their environment, the ways in which they negotiate the content and the practical arrangements, ultimately arriving at institutionalised procedures or not as the case may be, should make it possible to reply to a number of questions. What are the possible approaches to defining the concept of "community" in its relations with the university? How do these different approaches overlap, and how do they develop in regard to each other? To what extent does the search for and application of a particular dynamic imply that one favours this or that particular "model"? And finally, is there a geo-political forum (or fora) particularly suitable for bringing to the surface these reciprocal relationships and, if there is, on what conditions and under what constraints? This chapter has replied in the main to the first and second questions. In Part Two of this study we shall try to reply to the other two questions.

Chapter 4

STRATEGIES FOR UNIVERSITY-COMMUNITY RELATIONS

Whether to give greater importance to informal relations centred on individuals or to formalised institutional mechanisms; whether to use participative procedures which make it possible to initiate and regulate relations on a day-to-day basis, or to use medium and long-term planning (at national or regional level) — these are choices which, as we have seen earlier, depend on the different ways in which the term community is understood, and at the same time determine the global strategies which will be adopted for the development of those relations.

The attempt to clarify the concepts and identify the strategies must not be allowed to conceal the great variety of situations. But behind the differences in situations, mechanisms, and structures it is possible to discern a number of general trends and "official channels".

Flows of information — their volume, method of circulation, the media they use and the speed with which they work — are an important determinant of the intensity and nature, and even the possibility, of university/community relations. There are also a number of other factors which constitute the framework for such relations in practice.

The levels of development of the country in general and of the community concerned are particularly important. This is in our view an essential consideration, especially if the strategies we are describing are also to be applied to the developing countries. Close links between the university and the community, organised in the light of the practical problems to be solved, may be much more important for those countries than for the OECD Member countries. It is however difficult to establish an effective partnership in those countries, and there are obvious risks attached to an excessively one-sided subjection to a political authority or to economic interests which are bound to be multinational. The less developed the country or region is, the slighter are the chances of developing a multiple network on informal contacts, the greater the temptation for the university to withdraw into itself, and the more useful and necessary a co-ordinated central policy plan becomes.

The degree of centralisation in the country in question, i.e. its structural organisation and socio-political traditions, is another decisive factor. It determines the ways in which resources are pooled, whether this means the sharing of equipment and facilities, integration, or simply each side putting its resources at the other's disposal. It facilitates or renders inoperative the various kinds of consultative and co-operative mechanisms we shall describe in Part Two. It largely determines the method of allocating budget appropriations, the relative weights of the public and private sectors, and the relative importance of formal and informal relations.

A third general factor is the existence, or absence, of regional policies, whether these are of central origin or represent what other OECD studies have termed "internal" regional strategies. We dealt in some detail with the significance of this distinction in the previous chapter.

Another important factor is the way in which the different social forces in the various co-ordinating or co-operating bodies are represented, and the balance between them. In Sweden the trade unions, employers and the public authorities are always present together, while in other countries it is the public authorities which are almost always the main interlocutors, and in yet others the employers' associations.

To a more limited but no less important extent the forms of co-operation depend on the decision-making mechanisms. We shall return later (Part Two, Chapter 1) to the relative failure of arrangements for the participation of representatives of the community in the central management bodies of the universities. The types of decisions that these bodies traditionally have to take has not been adequately analysed, and this has resulted in some disappointment on both sides.

Finally, the importance of each of these factors varies considerably depending on the type of co-operative activity in question. The relative weights to be given to the level of development, the degree of centralisation, the scope and nature of regional policy, the distribution of social and political forces, etc., are bound to differ depending on whether one is dealing with applied research, training-employment regulation, action on behalf of under-privileged groups or regions, and so on.

In identifying these various factors therefore, we shall have to take an even closer look at the diversity of situations and mechanisms we have described. It would seem however that beyond the many differences it is possible to discern *a limited number of possible global strategies which are almost invariably found in combination with each other.* There would seem to be three general lines of approach, which we shall call planning strategy, alternation strategy and participation strategy.

These strategies emphasize different aspects of the problem. The first is basically operational, and amounts to a systematic approach to university-community relations. The second is more a practical and limited method of exchange centres on a essentially pedagogical process. The third has more of a political dimension and corresponds to the development of a certain type of democratic society. The fact is that each of them refers to a different conception of university-community relations, and above all to a different view of the changes to be made in the way university functions. The first two can be applied by universities still functioning on traditional lines, whereas the third may entail drastic changes.

Alternation strategy is based on a relatively static concept of relations between the university and its environment. It is designed to make a qualitative improvement in one of the services which the university provides for the community, namely better adjusted training for graduates.

Planning strategy is also based on what we have called an "instrumental" concept of higher education. It is much wider in scope than alternation strategy, and involves more complex procedures for mutual adaptation which although they lead to the creation of rational planning models, are coming under increasingly sharp criticism because of their inability to allow for the psychological and political dimensions of the environment and to propose really original models.

That, on the other hand, is precisely what participation strategies seem to do, at the risk indeed of being overwhelmed by psychological and political factors and finding great difficulty in formulating their objectives clearly and explicitly.

1. PLANNING STRATEGY

The crises that have recently come to affect industrialised societies — the energy crisis (leading to efforts to find new and independent sources and to reduce consumption), the crisis in currencies (inflation and exchange rates), unemployment, the decline in growth rates and even negative growth — have increased the importance of planning strategies but also deflected them in directions which may be considered retrograde. Economic objectives are now being drastically revised at the expense of cultural and social objectives, and there is a tendency to shelve measures to reduce inequalities and disparities and give priority to expansion and the concentrations which that sometimes necessitates.

In 1974 the OECD could still say [22]: "The regional problem is thus a combination of problems, economic, spatial and land use, social and environmental, all of which call for attention and none of which can be dealt with to the exclusion of the others. Since progress in one direction is dependent on progress in the others, to lay undue emphasis on any one element would be to oversimplify the nature of the regional problem. Individual countries give different weights to economic or social and environmental problems as they affect regions. In recent years, regional policies have been increasingly concerned not only with economic disparities but also with such problems as urban settlement, the overcoming of overcrowding and congestion of large cities, the decay of large city centres, the improvement of social conditions in disadvantaged regions or in regions of expansion, including housing, education and environment and 'quality' of life as well as the protection of the environment against industrial pollution, and the conservation of amenity areas. These objectives need to be fully integrated into those of regional policies as a whole which are thus either exclusively economic or exclusively social".

It is striking to see how today the bulk of efforts to improve university-community relations concern employment-training adjustments, vocational training and closer contacts with industry and the various production sectors.

This trend entails an apparent return to national planning, with reduced transfers to deprived areas, incentives for manpower mobility and greater emphasis on employment problems. However, the attempts of Member countries to adapt the educational system to society's demands and needs are no longer being made only at the level of society as a whole. There is a growing desire to gear higher education institutions more closely with their surrounding local and regional communities, establish stronger links, co-ordinate policies and respond to a constantly growing range of specific requirements and objectives.

Regional development policies themselves have several different objectives:
- Reduction of regional disparities (*objective of equality*) by among other things reducing the difficulties of physical access to educational facilities; this objective is achieved essentially through policies concerning the siting of university institutions;
- Alignment of curricula on regional needs and realities (*objective of adaptation and diversification*);
- Decentralisation and devolution of decision-making powers and mechanisms (*objective of participation*);
- Integration of education policies with the various sectoral policies with a view to land-use development and more efficient planning (*objective of improved efficiency*) [21].

These four main objectives may either be combined or pursued separately. A number of the institutional mechanisms we have described correspond to one or more of them.

Regional problems are not new. Quite apart from their administrative and political origins which go back to the emergence of independent states in most cases, they have developed in the wake of agricultural specialisation, the rapid growth of towns, and the spread of trade and industrial activities.

But for a long time the place of higher education in these policies was very modest, apart from technical and vocational training and the time-honoured example of the Land Grant Colleges (1863).

Examples of more recent developments are the following:

- Yugoslav resolution of 1960 on the training of technical personnel;
- The setting up in 1966 of the Instituts universitaires de technologie (IUT) in France;
- Spread of the Polytechnics in the United Kingdom;
- Regional Colleges in Norway;
- Regional Colleges plus National Institutes of Higher Education in Ireland.

In the universities in particular, many forces combine to slow down this attempt at adaptation and diversification. Teachers in higher education, employers and managers, students and parents used the idea of equal quality and equal validity to press for a homogeneous education system irrespective of the location and type of establishment which provided it.

The system of resource allocation, like the idea, frequent in Europe, of "national degrees", considerably slowed down any attempt at diversification at both the admission and graduation ends of the educational system. Indeed, one of the first concerns of the Open University in the United Kingdom was to guarantee that the degrees it awarded would be identical with those of the traditional universities.

In this context, therefore, the insistence that there must be community representatives on governing boards of universities, and the proliferation of bodies to ensure co-ordination with the community may be regarded as part of an approach to a more effective regional planning. The same may also be said of the emergence in nearly every country of "extension services" or "Missions de formation permanente". But, as a rule, the planning procedures are carried on "over the heads" of the university system and therefore do not lead to the setting up of special structures other than for co-ordination or the sharing out of tasks.

As regards research, participation in industrial or economic development, and the adjustment of training to employment — the main areas of planning strategy — it is usually at regional and central (or federal) levels that the decision-making and consultative bodies are set up.

Such bodies are particularly sensitive when it is a question of setting up university institutions, and the decision to do so sometimes looks more like an intervention to offset a trend it has not been possible to control rather than the product of real co-operation.

In such strategies, the place of education as a whole and higher education in particular is a subordinate one. In them, education is considered only in its "instrumental" aspect and is therefore significantly involved only in the technical and professional fields. Furthermore, such strategies endeavour to ensure that the national, regional and intra-regional levels are as closely articulated as possible.

It is only recently that the regional level has become particularly important. There would seem to be three main reasons for this:

- Quite apart from its specific functions of teaching and research, higher education is increasingly considered to be part of the network of public facilities:
    - it is a centre of attraction for individuals and for enterprises;
    - it modifies the qualifications structure of the supply side of the labour market;
    - it stimulates job creation;
    - it encourages mobility;
    - and it has own intrinsic social and cultural effects of a kind which is now described by the term "quality of life".

- It is easier to achieve a balance between education and employment at regional and interregional level; more generally, the region is a suitable context for harmonizing and monitoring a wide range of decisions and is consequently a more appropriate planning framework, because it is more limited in scale and more consistent.
- Precisely because they have expanded so fast, educational systems have been subjected to a growing concentration of decision-making powers, a proliferation of central services, and a widening of the gap between users and decision-makers, so that the central authorities themselves are increasingly in favour of administrative devolution, and the region seems to be the best level for co-operation between central, federal, local and other authorities.

However, since the local and regional authorities, especially those in disadvantaged regions, do not have enough political weight, regional policies — where they exist — are in fact, as we have already pointed out, "central" regional policies.

Their basic method of functioning is much more akin to co-ordination and surveillance than to consultation and negotiation. The increasing relationships between the university and its environment are therefore the necessary consequences, at the implementation stage, of a number of decisions. They are more concerned with procedures, methods and means than with the analysis of problems and the preparation of projects. They enable those who are not directly involved in carrying out the plan to remain uninvolved in its performance even though they are directly or indirectly affected by its consequences.

Constraints and obstacles

Planning strategies thus come up against a number of obstacles and create certain constraints. One of these is the preference inevitably given to formal rather than informal mechanisms, and to institutional responses rather than individual or non-permanent group responses. This may well render inoperative an important part of the university/community dynamic, hamper mutual adjustments, codify responses and aggravate conflicts of authority.

Another constraint, frequently stressed by participants at the Conference in February 1980, is the increased control and co-ordination "from above" at the expense of consultation and negotiation, and which runs counter to the decentralisation and diversification which the development of university/community relations seemed likely to promote.

Thirdly, the relationships between the development of higher educational institutions and regional development are far from univocal. In an article in the European Journal of Education, Guy Neave applies to the study of this relationship a typology worked out by Okun-Richardson, and comes to a very tentative conclusion [23].

Assuming that there are four types of regional situation:

- Low-income stagnant regions (LSRs),
- Low-income growing regions (LGRs),
- High-income stagnant regions (HSRs),
- High-income growing regions (HGRs),

the following situations may arise:

- In the LSRs the limited employment market gives rise to a strong demand for education, a relatively significant expansion in higher education, and this results in an increase in emigration and therefore a worsening of the initial situation;
- In the LGRs, the expansion in higher education may result in increased emigration, which may make growth more vulnerable;

— In the HSRs, the structure is more complex: because there is plentiful employment in jobs at low technological levels (these are generally mining, textiles and big steel producing regions) a large part of the population has a relatively low level of education, while the higher social groups have a very high rate of university enrolment;

— In the HGRs, university expansion would seem to go hand in hand with the development of an advanced economy, but since that usually takes the form of very complex enterprises and multinationals, neither the fallout effects nor the decisions they take really affect the region.

The planning models may well conceal these complex interactions and produce the opposite of what they intend. These analyses are moreover broadly confirmed by the experience of a great many developing countries, and by the part played by the universities in speeding up the "brain drain".

Finally, planning strategies, whether prepared at national or at regional level, are never able to settle all the conflicts and remove all the ambiguities. Planning procedures are generally defined according to the *priorities* revealed by analyses. But what does *priority* mean when applied, for example, to a particular sector of scientific research? Does it refer to the importance of that sector as regards the development of knowledge and theory? Or the urgency or seriousness of the problems depending for their solutions on the development of that sector: defence, health, energy? Or again, does it mean that the development of that sector is consistent with a number of deliberate political or social choices?

And, still taking as our example the field of scientific research, the rules for implementing the plans may be of quite different kinds. They may be based on systematic support for the most efficient and largest research teams, or on systematic support for the smallest teams so as to spread the work territorially and increase competition. They may involve the centralisation of resources at the risk of increasingly disassociating research from teaching, or the spreading of resources in accordance with a particular political or social choice. And so on.

In other words, instead of increasing the university's involvement in society, planning strategy may finally result in an authoritarianism which may be rational but can sometimes also be blind and inefficient.

This last remark brings us to yet another obstacle — the "autonomy" of the universities. The quality of the university's contribution to the community seems to be directly related to its ability to take decisions, to criticise, and to initiate action; in other words, to be autonomous. Here again, the danger is that the institution becomes completely subservient, and turns its back on its own objectives. The course of events in certain developing countries provides only too convincing proof of this: the subservience of the universities to government policies has in some instances gone a long way towards rendering them incapable of taking part in national development.

Finally, there is ample proof, as L. Cerych points out [24], of the ineffectiveness of proposing new objectives to the universities from a government decision-making sector. The reason for this seems to be neither the autonomy of the universities, since is often more ideological and intellectual than real, nor their "resistance to change", since that familiar phrase is more descriptive than explanatory, even though it is traditionally used by most sociologists of innovation. It is better to look for the reasons for this resistance in the complexity of the relations between the various actors within the university system, and the complexity of the relations that system has with the outside world. "Higher education in any country constitutes a social sub-system which itself consists of all the sub-systems (or complex organisations) represented by the different universities in the country in question. This national affiliation manifests itself through a system of relationships partly determined by the prevailing power structure (formal or informal) and partly by the behaviour of the actors (teachers, students, government departments, employers of graduates, etc.). This behaviour pattern is in its turn governed by historical traditions, the dominant values in each of the groups, the economic and political situation in the country in question, etc. Yet this complexity, which often has paralysing effects, also represents an opportunity for innovation."

It would not seem possible therefore to mobilise such complex structures and steer such different actors all in the same directions. Over-inflexible planning attempts therefore come to grief when they are confronted with the impossible task of simultaneously influencing so wide a range of factors, at the same time turning their backs on the opportunities for invention and change that such complexity and differences represent.

2. ALTERNATION STRATEGY

Alternation here means the systematic inclusion in the students' training course (but also in their teachers' working commitments) of periods of work in an enterprise, these periods of practical experience being closely co-ordinated with the teaching periods.

In relation to the whole range of possible relationships between university and community, alternation is only a partial strategy which mainly concerns teaching methods and the inclusion of services to the community in the student training process. It may therefore be regarded as a typical case of educational planning. But it stems from an original hypothesis which merits separate examination. For the advocates of alternation, the main problem in university-community relations is the *unsuitability of the courses* the university provides and *the fact that each side knows so little of the other*. The purpose of alternation is therefore to improve the courses and to reduce, if not eliminate, the lack of knowledge of each other. The same idea also underlies efforts to integrate town and university full-time teachers and practising professionals, and industrial and laboratory research, and the inclusion of members of the community on university boards or, in general, when any attempt is made to reduce distances and conflicts by bringing people with different personal experiences together.

Apart from the undoubted usefulness of developing alternation to facilitate new relationships between university and community, a number of more specific arguments can be advanced for encouraging the developments of such relationships:

— The democratisation of education: the possibility of engaging in higher studies immediately after secondary school is not provided equally to all students because of their social origins. Alternation arrangements would:
  — enable a university course to be preceded by a period of work in industry;
  — provide students with a way of themselves financing their studies;
  — shorten the real time devoted to studies (even though the total period to graduation might be longer);
— There would be a closer connection between theory and practice, which would facilitate the learning process, give it greater depth and eliminate the period of adjustment to working life once study has been completed;
— There would be a better provision of guidance for students since there would be no danger that students taking long courses might be unaware of the type of professional work (and the occupational context) they were preparing for;
— There could be a dialogue and a mutual understanding of problems between the university and its environment.

The introduction of contacts with the real world of industry and society in general implies changes along the lines of those outlined above in the teaching system but likely to go still further and bring about institutional modifications. On the community side (firms, regional and local authorities, etc.) arrangements to cater for students would enable them to obtain accurate information on the way the universities function so that exchanges between the two sides could proceed on a more objective basis.

Various forms of alternation

The history of alternation in education [25] shows that there have been several different models of alternation each of which has stressed one or other of the above arguments. We shall briefly recall here their main characteristics, beginning with the "co-operative education movement" initiated in 1906 by Herman Schneider at the University of Cincinnati. This movement had three objectives:

— A moral objective: to give students experience of the "natural law" of labour and hard work;
— A social objective: to enable poor students to pay for their own studies and secure subsequent employment (this was also the aim of the Northeastern University in Boston, set up in 1909 by Speare under the auspices of the YMCA) and thereby encourage the "survival of the fittest";
— A pedagogical objective: to make academic courses more relevant to the practice of a profession, and university study more consistent with occupational ambitions.

Nowadays, co-operative education appears to have abandoned the limitation to strictly work-oriented courses and includes "liberal arts studies" (in particular at Antioch College — since 1921). Although the "movement" comprised only 300 institutions and about 100 000 students in 1971, this type of alternation constitutes an important aspect of university strategy.

The second model is that of the "sandwich courses" in the United Kingdom. Although its origin goes back a long way (it was first applied in Bristol as early as 1878), this system is closely linked with the creation and development of the Polytechnics and hence with occupational types of education. whether it is a "thin sandwich" course (several short periods of work in industry interspersed with periods at a university) or a "thick sandwich" course (a single period of work per year or even one whole year of work in industry inserted after one or two years of study), the essential aim is to enable students to experience and get to understand the working world, help them to mature and develop a realistic outlook, and adapt them more effectively to the complex tasks they will have to carry out. During their periods at work, students keep in touch with their educational institution, which has usually arranged their "placing". They are visited two or three times by their "industrial tutor" and, especially when the period of work is organised in the form of a "project", they have to report to a joint panel consisting of their tutors and representatives of the firm.

"Study-Service" practices, albeit very different from the two preceding examples, which are systematic strategies, must still be regarded as a form of alternation. Later on (Part Two) we shall stress the very great variety of such practices, and the fact that they correspond more closely to a policy for relations with the community than the two preceding models. They are widely encountered in most English-speaking countries. In the United States, many students become voluntary social workers and their activities as such are partly credited as university study.

Finally, the development of continuing education in all OECD countries and especially the introduction of *educational leave* may be considered to come within the definition of a continuing education and training policy for workers and adults, and hence to be moving in the same direction as the alternation strategies proposed by the academic world for better adapted university teaching. We shall, however, deal later with the difference between these two approaches, and in particular the difference between the concepts of "alternation" and "recurrent education".

The concept of alternation between work and study may thus apply to many activities. In its most "organised" form it refers to the inclusion of "in-service" training periods in study time, whether these periods are exceptional or repeated at regular intervals. It is, for example, the "normal" form for medical study in most OECD countries, and for most technical study courses.

In certain cases, we can also speak of personally arranged, or "unofficial" alternation, when for example workers use all or part of their leisure time to take various types of courses (part-time, correspondence, evening courses, radio and television programmes, etc.). This type of alternation frequently precedes and is a necessary preliminary for transition to a situation of recurrent education — on which we shall have more to say later — e.g. through "educational leave". This is the case in Belgium, Italy and certain socialist countries, where the fact of having enrolled for evening classes and correspondence courses increases the entitlement to educational leave.

Obstacles and constraints...

The strategy of alternation can certainly not be used for the whole range of university-community relations, and encounters in practice a number of obstacles and constraints.

Firstly, alternation seems to function much more like a "pedagogical kit" than an original concept of university-community relations. even from the pedagogical standpoint, it is ambiguous on more than one count and consists in some cases of a mere succession or juxtaposition of activities in which the process of interaction is far from obvious.

Secondly, even when alternation seems to be central to an institution's policy, it is striking to see that it is never applied right across the board. In the first place, for reasons which are easily grasped, it can only be practised by full-time students. Whether in the British polytechnics or in an institution as specialised as Northeastern University, it is not applied to part-time students. It is not therefore a strategy of permanent or continuing education. In the second place, when it comes to training élites for the higher echelons of technology, the argument about the need for familiarity with shop-floor conditions loses its force and universality. The "Grandes Écoles" in France are of course increasing the number of internships in industry, but no one has yet thought of introducing them into the preparatory classes which are really the places where the élites are educated. in the Soviet Union, the obligation to participate in industry is dropped when students are being trained to work in the more advanced sectors.

Thirdly, contact with the community and industry during in-service training, especially when it is only for short periods, is sometimes artificial. In the larger firms, which are often the most outgoing, the view the student obtains of the way industry really works may well be fragmentary and naïve. The trainee is in an ambiguous position. Unless he is involved in a project, or has a certain autonomy, he may be complying with criteria which are more university-based than real. In other cases — and particularly in practices of the study-service type — one is struck by the latent "boy scout" mentality which turns students into voluntary social workers, no doubt satisfying their desire to be useful to society and establish contacts with reality, but at the risk of distorting their perception of the latter in more ways than one.

... and a confusion of two concepts

Finally, it is important to be clear about the difference between alternation and recurrent education. Alternation is based on a more or less authoritarian planning of the university curriculum by introducing a sequential system generally organised in advance. It is a strategy for improving the effectiveness of the teaching process and the preparation of students to meet the demands of working life. Recurrent education is an original policy for education which combines an employment policy, a social policy and a concept of teaching. As the OECD/CERI studies point out, "it argues not for new educational objectives but basically for an alternative of educational opportunity, where the present system is gradually transformed so that it no longer provides education in one stretch during the individual's youth, but over his whole lifetime and in alternation with other activities and in particular with work." [26]

A recent CERI study [27] lists as follows the principles of recurrent education as they were formulated in 1973:

— "The last years of compulsory education should provide a curriculum that gives each pupil a real choice between further study and work;
— After leaving compulsory schooling, access to post-compulsory education should be guaranteed to the individual at appropriate times over his total life-cycle;
— Distribution of facilities should be such as to make education available to all individuals as far as possible wherever and whenever they need it;
— Work and other social experience should be regarded as a basic element in admission requirements and curricula design;
— It should be possible to pursue any career in an intermittent way, alternating between study and work;
— Curricula design and content and teaching methodology should be designed in co-operation with the different groups involved (students, teachers, administrators, etc.) and adapted to the interests and motivations of different age and social groups;
— Degrees and certificates should not be looked upon as an "end result" of an educational career but rather as steps in a process of lifelong education, lifelong career and personality development;
— On completion of his compulsory education, each individual should be given a right to periods of educational leave of absence with the necessary guarantee for job security and social welfare".

This is therefore an open, comprehensive approach in which each individual is given the power to organise his own training, to choose the highest level of training he aspires to and the periods of his life when he wishes to be trained. Recurrent education also presupposes that special institutional mechanisms are set up and that every social, business, cultural or education institution is considered to be an effective learning centre. A policy of this nature is inseparably bound up with a profound social transformation and a change in the conditions of life in industry itself, and is therefore much more of a theoretical reference model than a clearly defined educational practice.

To revert to the metaphor of the sandwich courses, one could say that alternation strategy makes sure that the two kinds of training are not mixed — that the slices of bread are quite separate from the ham between them — while recurrent education is much more a strategy of interaction and mutual transformation, the long-term effects of which are however much less easy to keep track of.

In other words alternation is a deliberately limited strategy. It promotes relationships between one part of the university and the community. It protects the other parts of the university from contamination with reality. Whereas recurrent education is an open strategy which, as its name indicates, depends on the interaction between the passage through life in the community and the transformation of higher education structures.

3. PARTICIPATION STRATEGY

While the use of the term "participation strategy" seems very well suited for a number of situations and types of relationships, it can lead to misunderstandings:

— Of the three strategies it is certainly the one that is hardest to give formal expression to: it is in fact present at certain times both in planning procedures and in alternation mechanisms;

— Participation is not just a practical process for organising social relations, but also reflects a system of values and tends to function like a myth which is either passionately believed in, or rejected because of its unwieldiness or the risks it might entail in leaving responsibilities ill-defined.

Over the last ten years, and starting from a wide range of diferent, if not contradictory, points of view, a critical attitude has developed with regard to all the structures of society and its hierarchical pattern. In general, adults living and working in society are increasingly challenging the need to delegate their powers and claiming the right to participate in the decisions which affect them. Strangely enough, these criticisms have coincided with questioning of hierarchical and bureaucratic procedures by the sociology of organisations and the new theories of management.

In the struggle now developing between authority and participation in decision-making, the right of acces to knowledge, to education and to a wider training is vaguely emerging as a part of the answer. The university is not therefore just one of the places where these claims are being put forward, it is also one of the issues at stake. But the host of claims for improved social status through access to education and information far exceeds the capacities of university structures in the various countries. The maintenance of strongly hierarchical dependent relationships (among teachers, between teachers and students), the fact that teachers are recruited according to exclusively academic criteria, the pride of place accorded to the transmission of knowledge at the expense of analysis of situations, the refusal or inability to take into account what the surrounding community is doing, all these are phenomena which, far from making the university look like a possible provider of some of the answers to the problem, may well give it the appearance of a traditional fortress protected from the major cross-currents which activitate and mobilise the community, or make it into one of the places where those pressures conflict with the utmost violence.

Accordingly, the problem of participation may be considered from two different but interconnected viewpoints. The first is concerned with the relations of the university with the surrounding community — its degree of autonomy and the nature of that autonomy vis-à-vis the central government or the various structures of political, economic and other power — and the forms of interaction between the various component parts of the social system and the university institution. The second considers the problems of the internal democratisation of the university, the decision-making mechanisms, and the new management procedures which have been introduced in certain Member countries. We are concerned here with the first of these approaches, but we shall have more to say later on the difficult relationships emerging between democratisation, autonomy and community participation.

Some operating principles

Firstly, participation strategy reflects an approach to the community which is not so much geographical and administrative as structural. It is based on identification of the different groups making up the community and the different functions they perform. Depending on the case, it gives pride of place to local communities or to certain sectors of activity (public sector, enterprises, "communities of interest", social and political structures).

Secondly, participation strategy tends to give special importance to the university's local and regional activities. This does not mean that the university abandons its national and international vocations. But the emphasis put on the concepts of region, community and clearly defined social groups means deliberately directing the activities of the higher educational institutions towards certain practical problems. At the same time it involves the deliberate narrowing of the scope of all or some of those activities by choosing to promote them where they can have immediate effect, i.e. in the systems where individuals and communities can immediately reinvest any acquired abilities at their own level. It also makes possible inter-sectoral and co-ordinated activities with other institutions working on the same scale, permits the participation of those at whom the action is aimed, and leads to concentration on situations where the feedback is sufficiently immediate to allow its effects to be controlled.

On the one hand there is a search for a more direct and verifiable efficiency, a fuller acceptance of social and political responsibiliy, But there is also a desire to keep track of the consequences of one's action — which is one meaning of the celebrated slogan "small is beautiful". Graduates, students and teachers seem less anxious than their elders to change the world, and in this respect they are noticeably different from their counterparts in the '60s, and more concerned to do something about their environment. This is interpreted in some quarters, particularly in countries like France or Germany, as a relative depoliticisation of the university in comparison with the great movements of 1968, *whereas it is really a matter of change of scale and of methods of political analysis.*

Thirdly, participation strategy tends to give special prominence to all consultation and negotiation practices. The planning of research and teaching activities has generally been based on models of a deductive type. Both the elaboration of research programmes and proposals for new curricula are still generally the direct product of the state of previous knowledge viewed in the context of the budgetary and human resources available. They therefore lead to more or less authoritarian decisions as to distribution, and a *de facto* control of the development of relations between the university and the community.

The development of "participatory" relations with the community usually leads to the practice of "negotiated programming". This is particularly apparent in the case of the various fields of education. When they provide continuing training, and indeed initial training, higher education institutions are sometimes obliged to negotiate veritable training contracts covering content and methods as well as numbers of people to be trained, either with the regional or local authorities, or with enterprises of potential employers (including administrations) or with the trainees themselves.

In some countries consultation on training programmes and curricula is made compulsory by law and by financial procedures (Belgian Act on continuing training, French Act of 1971, and the regulations in most American States). In all these cases, whenever it is a question of voluntary students registered who are members of recognised occupational or cultural groups but not working for a degree or studying for promotion in their job, there is systematic negotiation of content and methods between the students and the university in which the demands and needs of these members of the community are genuinely taken into account.

This *consultation criterion* implies that higher education institutions will *accept supervision* of their activities *by the community*, but also that the community will agree to the discussion of its requests, whether these relate to vocational training, continuing training, adult education, or even research or management. Because of its repercussions therefore the very *fact of negotiation* is of the highest importance.

The repercussions involved are indeed important for the operation of the universities themselves. Inasmuch as these negotiating processes entail innovation and change, they cease to be a mere pedagogical innovation aiming at more or less illusory improvements in teaching efficiency, and become *a dynamic link between higher education and its environment which creates an obligation to innovate and supports and fosters change.* It can therefore be presumed that the development of relations with the community induces in institutions a type of pedagogical and social change which is both more coherent and more lasting, i.e. better suited for general application independently of the groups which initiate them and less vulnerable to the traditional process by which innovations that are purely endogenous to the university system become obsolescent.

Obstacles and constraints

As in the case of the two other strategies described above, we must now see what obstacles and constraints are encountered in attempts to manage university-community relations on a participation basis.

In spite of their flexibility and the seeming ease with which they can be got going, all participation strategies are unwieldy and fraught with difficulties.

Obstacles to decision-making

In practice, participation poses some very delicate if not insoluble problems of management, and generally slows down decision-making considerably. It depends very much on a precarious balance of forces and therefore involves an enormous effort of clarification and consultation which those involved usually have neither the time, the desire, nor the means to undertake.

Confusion of concept and practice

If some forms of alternation have been described as "sandwich" courses, some forms of university teaching which must be included under participation ought to be called "hotchpotch" courses, because it is so difficult to identify their ingredients. They are ill-defined mixtures of field work, university studies, research, pragmatic methods, individual work, group work, systematic analysis and intuition. Many of the most popular attempts at extra-mural work of on-the-spot field work merit this scepticism, in spite of the interest and enthusiasm they arouse in students, sometimes in teachers, and less often among community bodies. In other words, certain systems of multiple interaction between university and community often result in ill-defined relationships from which neither side stands to gain. Academics, and intellectuals generally, find it difficult to move around in the community "like a fish in water".

Difficulties of control and evaluation

Owing to the many feedback effects and the complexity of university-community relations, it is very difficult to evaluate the impact of a participation strategy and to control it in operation, especially since participation is generally assumed to take place at all levels. One of the characteristic features of the university system and the social system as a whole, is that side by side with areas which are being increasingly democratised, other areas are developing along increasingly hierarchical lines. It is striking to observe, for example, that in certain European countries the claim that the universities are being given an increasing measure of autonomy has been accompanied by the development of techniques for rationalising budget choices or meticulously devised system of norms which largely cancel out the effects of that autonomy. Moreover, in a system of participatory management, activities are always planned on the basis of a comparison of needs and choice between those needs, and not on the basis of a comparison of input with results, which in fact means that an evaluation of the results cannot be taken into account.

Participation by and with the community, and "internal participation"

As pointed out at the beginning of this chapter, it is not so easy to reconcile the consequences of participation by the community in university affairs with those arising from an increasing measure of internal participation, i.e. the democratisation of university management, and participation by all grades of teachers, students and personnel in decision-making.

The study carried out by Jean Jadot for the Programme on Institutional Management on Higher Education Conference brings out the following facts, which are not as contradictory as they would seem. The more autonomy universities have, and the greater their ability to use this autonomy to operate as full partners in the various community bodies, the less talk there is of participation by all in decision-making. On the other hand, it is precisely in universities with the least autonomy that participation in the sense of internal democracy — has developed the most and led to the emergence of new powers, i.e. those of the students and the staff. But although these new powers are not opposed — quite the opposite — to the traditional public service functions of education and research, they do very little to help the university assert itself in a competitive context or to enable it to engage in flexible interpenetration with the community.

The limitation of university autonomy does not affect the academic freedom of teachers — or of students — in the choice of their subjects or in the teaching methods they regard as most suitable, but it can reduce the ability of universities to develop a growing variety of strategies and to respond to necessarily fluctuating and sometimes contradictory demands.

The main difficulty with a participation strategy is that it immediately raises the problem of autonomy, both for the university and for its partners in the community. But that may also constitute its chief virtue. Like the model of recurrent education, with which it has much in common, participation strategy is not only a strategy for solving problems but is also, unlike planning and alternation strategies, an ambitious model which necessitates consideration of the possibility of internal democracy in the university on the one hand, and the possibility of industrial democracy and the development of associative and democratic forms at all levels in the community on the other. It is obviously a utopian model, but its dynamic potential may prove as interesting as its immediate results.

CONCLUSION

The lengthy — but by no means exhaustive — analysis we have made of the three strategies shows the difficulties of developing university-community relations and the requirements that are implicit in the process.

It is indeed necessary to go further and recognise that the dynamic of those relations is such that sooner or later one of the partners (the university or the community) will begin to adopt defensive attitudes or try to dominate the process by taking over the instruments of decision-making. A further obstacle to attempts to develop such co-operation is the tendency to prefer formal mechanisms and institutional responses to informal mechanisms and responses by individuals or non-permanent groups. In other words an ossification of relations may develop and hence render reciprocal adaptation difficult.

A deliberately open-minded attitude in this respect is all the more necessary since planning efforts may very often, with the best of intentions, result in a reinforcement of structures and mechanisms at the expense of diversification and flexibility. Whilst it may be accepted that one of the crucial contributions the university can make to the development of the community is its ability to make decisions and criticise, there is a danger that over-emphasis on efforts to plan — and institutionalise — university-community relations may result in the universities being tied down to socio-economic development policies which have been elaborated outside their precincts.

Thus, while it is necessary to develop reciprocal relationships, it is also essential, if only because of the very complexity of those relationships, to maintain a capability for innovation and change. A relationships structure must be found that is neither a hollow shell nor a rigid straight-jacket — and that is not easy to do.

The alternative would be to refuse to confine the definition of the university's environment to a territorially delimited area, however far that might extend. It would be necessary to insist on the absolute necessity of taking the environment into account in order to maintain the interactions necessary for the development of an open university system, but nevertheless consider it as a "variable geometry" environment depending on the types of action, the circumstance prevailing when the action takes place, and the strategies chosen.

69

Part Two

METHODS AND PROCEDURES
FOR UNIVERSITY-COMMUNITY RELATIONS

Chapter 1

TOWARDS A RECIPROCAL UTILISATION OF UNIVERSITY AND COMMUNITY RESOURCES

Utilisation by the university and the community of each other's resources is one of the main ways in which the university can respond to the expectations and needs of the community and to the pressures it exerts. The apparent agreement which emerged from the preparatory studies and the conclusions of the Conference in February 1980 as to the need for a reciprocal opening-up of human and material resources in fact conceals some ambiguity in that it may reflect any of three different approaches:

— The first is concerned with democratisation: to ensure that the university will not cater solely for a privileged group but will be open to all social categories, through continuing education, general education for the population, problem-oriented research and direct service to the community;

— The second is aimed at economic efficiency, i.e. the optimum utilisation of premises, equipment and manpower. This economic objective is particularly important during the present period of recession and cuts in resource allocations to the universities;

— The third relates to teaching techniques, and is designed to make teaching courses and research more appropriate to real needs: teaching in the field, closer links between the university and the business world through greater mobility of teachers and students, and the development of a new relationship between theory and practice.

Depending on the approach adopted, preference will be given either to human resources or to material resources and technical and scientific competence. Furthermore, these three approaches may result in the choice of different types of partners in the community. It is clear, however, that the three approaches do not conflict with each other but can be applied simultaneously in the context of a joint opening-up policy pursued by the university and the community together.

1. UTILISATION BY THE COMMUNITY OF THE UNIVERSITY'S HUMAN RESOURCES

Which of its human resources can be of benefit to the community?

The university's human resources are of two kinds: the teaching staff and research workers, and the students.

The large-scale use of teachers and researchers calls for no special comment, since virtually all universities which develop activities for the community do so with the help of teaching staff and researchers.

It would be necessary to go more deeply into the matter by distinguishing between teachers regularly involved in institutionalised activities, such as certain continuing education schemes, and teachers involved part-time in training, research and practical activities as required by the community in specific circumstances and for a specific duration. However, in some countries a policy for reintegrating academic staff into the community for the benefit of both sides is beginning to take shape. For example, in Sweden, teachers are sent to firms for variable periods of up to a year, without receiving any compensating allowances. The general trend is towards the tentative organisation of an alternation system for teachers and research workers. Finally, it must not be forgotten that many teachers are individually involved in the affairs of the community, which thus benefits from their experience and skills.

Utilisation of students is a more recent phenomenon, at least in some countries. The use of students in the context of university-community relations means taking the view that students represent an important potential resource for the community — one which, to the detriment of both the students and the community, is rarely or inadequately used. Alternation courses were originally thought of as the application of a theory taught at the university, the aim being to give students a more realistic and appropriate education. There have always been — in somewhat rudimentary forms perhaps — training courses in firms and other forms of contact with aspects of the business world and social reality. Some sectors, such as engineering, architecture and medicine, have a privileged position in this respect.

Medical studies are an interesting example. The university's assumption of responsibility for hospitals has enabled its students to render services directly related to their training. But the university has concentrated more and more on training specialists (at the hospital) to the detriment of general medical practice and other activities in the health sector. Direct service has thus given way to training through observation of the operations the specialist carries out at the hospital — a situation which has prompted countless satirical caricatures. Hence the tendency in certain medical universities [27] to involve the students at a very early stage in activities concerned with prevention, health education or primary health care delivery within the compass of the training stage they have reached.

This trend can also be seen in other areas. The initiation of students into working life is not only in the interest of the student but also of the community. At the Conference in February 1980, several speakers from Finland, Canada and France pointed out that the periods spent by undergraduates in small and medium-sized firms could offer opportunities for a very rewarding relationship. Guy Denielou, in his report to the Conference on the University-Industry working group, pointed out that "neither the employer nor the student is in a position of undue superiority, the one because he is too young and the other because he is not as knowledgeable as all that. It might to some extent be said that the undergraduate can do as much for technology as the mosquito does for malaria: he can innoculate it into some firms...". However this traditional alternation-type arrangement corresponds more to the third approach (improved teaching techniques), whereas the use of student resources to benefit the community is inspired rather by the first "democratisation" type of approach. Students can and should render services to the community and in particular to under-privileged groups, and these services can and should be integrated into their programmes of studies.

In this connection, the trend developing in some countries towards the organisation of "study service" deserves to be stressed. Thus two UNESCO General Conferences (in 1976 and 1978) have urged member countries to collect information about and promote study service, which is defined as "the involvement of students and staff in higher education in meeting human needs as an integral part of their courses".

Similarly, in the United Kingdom, a two-year project funded by the Department

of Education and Science began in February 1978. The Study Service Project defined study service as follows:
- Students (not staff) are involved;
- The work is an integral part of the curriculum — and preferably assessed;
- There is direct contact between students and beneficiaries;
- The effect of the work is detectable at individual and small-group level.

A voluntary organisation (the Community Service Volunteers: CSV) has made a wide survey of institutions of higher education in order to make known and promote study service activities. It recorded 223 activities in various fields. The following examples from the list drawn up by Peter Lewis and Carol Summers in 1978-79 illustrate the diversity and usefulness of the social commitment of students in the context of their studies:

Adult Education (5 projects)
> University of London: Assistance to community group in setting up radio station

Agriculture/Horticulture/Landscape Planning (9 projects)
> Somerset College of Agriculture and Horticulture: Design of village playground and planning of gardens for old people's flats...

Architecture (9 projects)
> Mackintosh School of Architecture, Glasgow: Assistance in building a leisure centre for the handicapped

Art and Interior Architecture (19 projects)
> Loughborough College of Art and Design or Winchester School of Art: Internal decoration in hospitals, prisons, ceramics with elderly people, etc.

Careers (12 projects)
> Paisley College of Technology: Advice to school leavers on placement

Construction (12 projects)
> Highbury Technical College, Portsmouth: Building of youth clubs with unemployed school leavers

Drama (5 projects)
> University College, Cardiff: Use of drama to assist language teaching with immigrant children

Engineering (13 projects)
> Nearly all these projects use simple methods to help the handicapped Kingsway Technical College, Dundee: Design and construction of special chairs for handicapped children, or Warwick University: Tactile mobility maps for use by blind people

General/Liberal Studies (13 projects)
> Jacob Kramer College of Art and Design: Organisation of holidays for handicapped people

Home Economics (5 projects)
> Queen Margaret College, Edinburgh: Assistance to elderly, young mothers on nutrition education and food budgeting

Librarianship 3 projects)
> Leeds Polytechnic: Help to users of the library for various searches

Management/Business Affairs (6 projects)
> University of Lancaster: Assistance in the marketing policy of community groups dealing with arts and training

Mathematics/Computing/Statistics (6 projects)

Leicester Polytechnic: Transportation surveys for city transport authority

Medicine/Nursing (16 projects)

Liverpool University: Students attached to a family as part of a course

Science (8 projects)

University of Essex: Undergraduate research projects of amino-acid composition of subnormal patients

Sociology (21 projects)

Socio-psychological projects from numerous universities for minorities and marginals

Teacher Training (26 projects)

Students teach in their own particular field of studies East Sussex College of HE: Students in physical education are used as monitors for a swimming club for handicapped children

Miscellaneous (43 projects)

Covering other sections such as veterinary medicine, hygiene, music, communication, nature conservation, etc.

The examples given above illustrate a new trend the educational and pedagogical consequences of which are obvious for all institutions, except for a few which persist in rejecting, for reasons which are not too clear, this kind of involvement on the part of their students.

In its issue of November 1978, "Community Service Volunteers" gives extracts from three unfavourable replies:

"As a learned institution we are not in a position to offer any constructive report..."

"I was asked to inform you that it was considered that it would not be appropriate for medical students to be included in the enquiry..."

"It is not part of the function of an educational institution to consciously take part in activities of this kind — people come here to study engineering."

In conclusion two further points about the use of student resources in higher education/community relations should be noted:

- The practice is considerably more developed in English-speaking and Scandinavian countries;
- It is more common in non-university post-secondary institutions, although a trend has recently emerged towards a more balanced distribution of responsibilities between the two sectors.

The community also has human resources at its disposal

Utilisation by the university of human resources from the community can take two different forms — the involvement of representatives of the community in the administration of the university, and the use of active professional people as teachers.

Participation by the community in university administration

Most of the universities in the United States, the United Kingdom, Canada and Sweden have for some time now had on their various committees members who are elected or nominated by various community authorities, and this trend is becoming more widespread.

But the significance of such arrangements must not be exaggerated. Their effectiveness is limited in at least three ways.

The first is the scope of the decision-making area in which members of the community are allowed to participate. They usually sit on bodies whose responbilities are essentially financial and administrative and, as a rule, have no right to consider or say anything about curricula matters, research programmes or the appointment of members of staff. For example, the University of Dijon (France) makes the point that "administrative details are of little interest to the members of the Council who care more about overall goals and plans of action...". In a few exceptional cases, however, there is active participation in the establishment of curricula, as for instance at the University of Bayreuth (Federal Republic of Germany): "the syllabus for the course in industrial management was worked out by a committee of representatives of the University, regional business and industry, and regional government".

The second limiting factor is the kind of people who represent the community. These are usually well-known local figures coming from business firms, local administration or management agencies, or certain professions. Almost all of them are likely to be graduates of higher education themselves. Paradoxically, their presence on the various university boards may actually reinforce the élitist aspects of higher education. This is not always the case, however, as the example of the City College of the City University of New York (United States) shows. In its Biomedical Program, the Community Advisory Committee was composed "not simply of physicians but of both professional and lay persons".

The third limiting factor has to do with the real nature of outside participation, including the nomination procedures. In practice, the co-option of leading figures from the outside world has often been the result of arbitrary decisions taken centrally which reflect no request either from the institutions or the community side.

Certain studies submitted to us do, however, attest to real community participation. To continue with the example of the City College of the City University of New York (United States), "members of this Committee did not hesitate to involve themselves — sometimes acrimoniously — in the affairs of the new Biomedical Centre, including student admissions, student academic standing, and the appointment and retention of staff"... The whole matter had ultimately to be taken to a court of law.

If representatives of the Community are consulted, they naturally need to feel that some account is taken of their opinions. Otherwise they tend to lose interest, as this example from the experience of the University of New England (Australia) shows: "the Professorial Board has recently made decisions directly contrary to recommendations from the Board of Continuing Education that were initiated by community members. The effect has been for the community members to come to see their participation as 'window-dressing' and a waste of their time." Should one conclude from this that the intrusion of the outside world may prove a threat to the University and a bringing into question of a solidly established system?

The utilisation of people in professional practice

Engineers, doctors, architects, lawyers and other professional people who put their experience and their knowledge of social, economic and cultural realities at the disposal of the university undoubtedly help to make the university system better fitted to meet real needs. Admittedly, this collaboration raises problems, but these can generally be overcome, as has been seen in certain universities for many years past. Such arrangements do not in fact constitute a challenge to academic knowledge and competence, but rather a different approach to problems.

The case is quite different when it comes to attempts to take account of other forms of knowledge available to the community which do not obey the rules governing the production of academic knowledge, and which may even challenge that knowledge, but also supplement and enrich it. It is less of a risk for a faculty of medicine to use a general practitioner to give the students a few lectures than to use the knowledge of a specialist in acupuncture, even if he is of equal professional status. There are in France some 4 000 specialists in acupuncture who are doctors, but acupuncture is not officially taught in faculties of medicine. This is because it is not a subject for academic research, and it cannot become a subject for academic research until it is recognised.

There are many instances of this kind of situation in which effective practice precedes university teaching. The acceptance by the university of a form of empirical knowledge is thus seldom possible.

It goes without saying that the use of the community's traditional skills, even when they are carried on by people without formal training or diplomas, is much more widespread and important in the developing countries. Quite apart from the "Chinese model", efforts have been made in certain countries such as Pakistan, the Philippines and Mozambique to set up cultural and technical lines of communication in the universities in order to be able to call on the immediately available resources of the community and help to develop applied technologies and local innovation capacities.

2. RECIPROCAL UTILISATION OF FACILITIES

Utilisation of university facilities by the community

These kinds of arrangements can range from access to libraries or the use of premises for lectures, meetings and other events to the use of laboratories, television, data-processing equipment and sports facilities or the consultation of various publications. Two things can be said about such arrangements:

- They do not arouse any serious conflictual problems — unlike certain cases where human resources are used — since they are unlikely to bring into question the university's goals and functions;
- They are — once again — much more frequent in the English-speaking countries. An example is the research undertaken by the Architectural Study Unit of University College, London [29], the aim of which was "to discover the links being established between polytechnics and their neighbourhoods, with particular emphasis on the sharing of physical resources".

The survey in question covers the following resources:

- General purpose teaching spaces;
- Specialised teaching spaces (laboratories; studios, etc.);
- Libraries and audio-visual centres;
- Computer centres;
- Spaces for social and recreational purposes (assembly halls, bars, theatres, exhibition galleries);
- Refectories;
- Indoor and outdoor sports facilities;
- Administrative spaces;
- Other spaces (bookshops, banks, medical centres, etc.).

The author of the survey report gives many examples of the ways in which polytechnics are putting their space and facilities at the disposal of the community. "In fact one of the strongest impressions gained after talking to so many people is that of a remarkable amount of good will and ingenuity devoted to offering resources to as many people as possible. But the author goes on to point out that the polytechnics often have great difficulty in providing for their own needs because their facilities are already inadequate.

To quote again from a submission from the United Kingdom, the Committee of Vice-Chancellors and Principals of the Universities point out that "the university becomes a centre for discussion and debate by groups of all political and philosophical persuasions and democratisation of access is enhanced by public lectures, meetings and exhibitions. Access by the public to particular academic areas such as libraries and laboratories is unlikely to be refused when the individual's reasons are sound, although this would in the main be reserved to outside scholars."

While in the United Kingdom the polytechnics seem to use their facilities to the maximum, for their own needs and for those of the community, in some other countries such facilities are by no means utilised to capacity: "...it must be remembered that in many universities internal sharing of resources already presents great difficulties and we all know cases of unnecessary duplication of electronic scanning microscopes, for instance" (Report to the Conference by the University-Industry Working Group). This under-utilisation is rendered worse in some cases when the universities are completely closed during vacation periods.

...but also the utilisation of community facilities by the university

Two main kinds of facilities are of interest here — community infrastructures, and the premises in which industrial or professional activities take place.

Utilisation of community infrastructures, and in particular the premises and equipment coming under the local and regional authorities, is less widespread than might be supposed. The only things frequently shared are sports equipment, theatres and sometimes libraries. Thus an agreement was concluded between the University and the Municipality of Rome concerning the use of the sporting facilities under construction in the Tor di Quinto quarter over a 92 000 sq.m. area. Under this agreement, the University of Rome will grant the use of the facilities to all students enrolled for an average period per month representing 20 per cent of the total operating time of all installations.

The Blocry Sports Centre at Louvain-la-Neuve (Belgium) is also a good example of the joint use of facilities in the context of new university-community relationships. In 1971, an agreement in principle was signed between the Belgian Government, the sports authorities and the universities on the basis of the following aims:

— The importance of co-ordinating government and university building programmes;
— The importance of joint management to ensure optimum utilisation of facilities;
— The need for closer co-operation between the government and the universities in the following fields: scientific research applied to sports, sports medicine and medical supervision of top-ranking sportsmen;
— The provision of administrative facilities and grants for student sportsmen of international level so as to enable them to carry on their academic studies and their sports training simultaneously; the desirability of an association with the Commune of Ottignies.

The agreement provided for a joint plan to build a very large sports complex (12 hectares of open-air sports facilities, 1 building housing 14 000 m² of games areas, 2 swimming pools) the financing of which would be shared jointly by the government, the universities and the commune in decreasing order of size of share. The joint management would be carried out by a non-profit-making association which would include representatives of the government, the universities and the commune in its decision-making bodies.

Furthermore, a tendency is clearly emerging to create and use facilities jointly in other sectors requiring increasingly sophisticated and costly equipment. This is happening in the industrial research sector, for example. Universities are increasingly finding that they are unable to provide research equipment and renew their technical infrastructure out of their normal budget.

In Germany, for example, the German Research Council (DFG) finds that scientists are increasingly including in their applications requests for major equipment which it would once have been thought normal for the university itself to provide. In some countries, both the research councils and, where they exist, private foundations have attempted to help universities in the maintenance of well-equipped laboratories.

On the other hand, certain firms and industries are anxious to limit the considerable investment required for this kind of equipment, which tends to become obsolescent quite rapidly. Hence the many bio-industrial laboratories and data-processing centres which are jointly run. Sometimes integration is carried a very long way, as for instance between the University of Delft and the Philips Company at Eindhoven in the Netherlands. When facilities are not available, some universities set up their own companies which purchase equipment, operate it on business lines and rent it back to the university on good terms. This is the case, for instance, with the Technological University of Loughborough (United Kingdom), which has set up a company called "Loughborough Consultants Ltd." to exploit the University's know-how and facilities. Since 1978, when this University acquired an Auger Spectrometer, the company was able to market successfully the expertise and equipment. The company decided to lease an ESCA instrument (Electronic Spectroscopy for Chemical Analysis) at the end of 1979 making available time to the University and selling a sufficient amount of instrument time to cover at least the costs of owning and operating the facility.

The use by the university of external industrial and professional facilities situated within the university's sphere of influence enables a new educational environment to be defined. Thus, there are numerous examples of teaching and research activities carried on in industrial laboratories, in primary and secondary schools for teacher training (which is no recent innovation), and primary, secondary or tertiary health care centres for the training of health personnel: dispensaries, community health centres, general practioners' surgeries, private hospitals and "university hospitals".

Some countries, such as the United States and the United Kingdom, are trying to innovate intensively in this respect by creating in the industrial sector the equivalent of university hospital centres in the field of medicine. These are virtual "industry-university centres" for teaching and research which also provide a solution to the problem of rapid changes in expensive equipment. The Committee of Vice-Chancellors and Principals of the Universities of the United Kingdom has, for example, stated that, with the aim of encouraging the development of a closer understanding between universities and manufacturing industry in the United Kingdom, the Science Research Council and the Government Department of Industry decided jointly in 1976 to launch the "teaching company scheme". Under this scheme a teaching company programme is undertaken jointly by a manufacturing company and a university or polytechnic. Each programme consists of an agreed set of tasks aimed at achieving a significant improvement in the company's manufacturing methods through close co-operation between the management of the company and the academic staff of the university or polytechnic. Graduate "teaching company associates" are employed, normally on two-year university contracts, to work within the company-academic team, learning from expertise in the company and in the university, taking part in supporting studies and contributing their own personal skills to the programme. It is envisaged that on completion of their tasks the associates should be ready for posts of responsibility in manufacturing engineering and management. Their salaries for the duration of the teaching company programme are met jointly by the Science Research Council and the Department of Industry. Some 20 programmes have so far been approved.

3.   OBSTACLES AND CONSTRAINTS

The reciprocal utilisation of both human and material resources therefore seems to be growing fast. However, when university resources are used by the community, the difficulties that arise are not of the same order as when community resources are used by the university. In the latter case, and particularly as regards human or scientific resources, a number of difficulties are raised, on the grounds that the use of community resources might endanger the independence and status of higher education.

The consensus is general when it comes to *using the resources of the universities*. The survey we made showed that 132 institutions, or 80 per cent of those contacted, considered that they placed their teaching staff at the disposal of the community, 88 institutions — or 60 per cent — allowed certain facilities or infrastructures to be used, and 60 (41 per cent) mentioned activities where students themselves were active in the community.

A distinction has to be made between the occasional or partial provision of facilities or staff, and situations implying full-time work or complete integration. For instance, the use of premises can range from access to the library and the loan of meeting rooms or lecture halls outside university hours, to the use of laboratories, television equipment or the time-sharing of computers, etc.

The use by higher education institutions of community resources would appear to be not so well developed. The results of our survey showed that only 36 per cent of the institutions consulted used community facilities for their teaching and research, apart from for traditional arrangements such as the use of hospitals for the training of health personnel and schools for training teachers.

As mentioned above the only elements frequently shared are sports facilities and meeting rooms. This may perhaps be due to the fact that as most university resources, and capital equipment in particular, are increasingly supplied by the state, it does not occur to anyone that they should be used in such a way as to maximise the return on them. Furthermore, administration structures work in watertight compartments, and have separate budgets, and no state agency would be prepared to suggest that its own budget should be reduced because it could use premises or equipment others had had built or assembled. In other words, it is sometimes because relations between the different community agencies and bodies are difficult or non-existent that higher educational institutions find it hard to co-operate with them.

The use of people working in industry or the professions as teachers or research staff seems to raise at least two other important questions:

— The status of such people when they become teachers, and the part they are to play in the decision-making structures;
— The possibility that the introduction of external skills more directed towards the solution of practical or concrete problems may bring into question the knowledge taught in universities.

Difficulties seem to arise in disciplines concerned with economic activities (management, finance, industry). In other disciplines, such as the humanities and the law, practitioners from the community are sometimes treated as outsiders because they are not members of the academic caste.

Similarly, in medicine, the use of a general practitioner as a teacher, for example, will hardly be accepted by some university specialists. All the more so, since the medicine actually practised by certain professionals without formal medical qualifications is not yet taught at the university and does not enjoy official recognition by it. Many other examples might be given. Students were familiar with the names of Marx and Freud from current usage in the community around them at a time when the university dared not mention their names. Technologies can have reached quite an advanced stage before being recognised by the university establishment.

The cultural or professional practices of the community therefore do not play as full a part as they could in the advancement of knowledge. In other words, the presence of practitioners from industry and professional life could be accepted, but only on condition that it was not institutionalised, since practitioners have a way of looking at problems which is necessarily quite different from that of academics.

CONCLUSION

Two other important points remain to be mentioned. The first is the location of the university, which we have already dealt with (see Part One). If universities are located in campuses which lie outside the economic, social and cultural activities of the community, it is very difficult for them to take part in this exchange of human and material resources. Secondly, there is the important problem of the exchange of information between the two parties concerned. The Conference of Rectors of West German Universities had the following to say about this:

"The exchange of material and human resources between institutions of higher education and the community is the result of needs which exist on either side. However, this kind of exchange will not reach its objectives unless both sides are sufficiently and constantly informed of what is available and what is required, whether of a material, human or scientific nature. This kind of permanent mutual information system is being developed in German institutions of higher education". In the United States, the United Kingdom, the Scandinavian countries, Belgium and France, "community liaison officers" and "public relations/information officers" are beginning to appear, together with information services and other staff responsible for circulating information.

These information systems are still not far enough developed. They constitute a major element in relations between the university and the community.

Chapter 2

VARIETY OF SPECIAL BODIES SET UP
TO DEAL WITH UNIVERSITY-COMMUNITY LINKS
AND COMMON PROBLEMS

Exchanges have always existed between the university and the community through contacts between individuals. These however have traditionally been comparatively rare and confined to a one-way flow of private individuals from higher education to the community. Thus, teachers and students may participate as individuals in the life and the development of the community, as members of local or municipal councils, as local or national elected representatives, as members or counsellors of various associations, as trade unionists, as participants in day-to-day operations and management for firms, or as contributors to research outside the university. In some Member countries and institutions a flow in the opposite direction of private individuals from the community to higher education has been initiated, e.g. people in active working life being invited to participate in teaching at the university, as we saw in the preceding chapter.

Pressure from the community, the urge for wider contacts and discussions, the desire to improve the quality of education and research, and the need to obtain new resources have led certain universities to set up a number of specific bodies which often complement existing arrangements for university-community interaction through the reciprocal utilisation of resources, community participation in the administration of the university and decision-making, and finally alternating education and research – one of the strategies for furthering university-community relations.

The type of liaison structures, their relative weight and the way they fit in with the general structures of the university largely determine the nature of university-community relations.

– Some broad trends can be distinguished:
  The creation of specific bodies to negotiate with the community, preferably separate from academic and research structures, and enjoying almost total autonomy in their management, financing and recruitment of staff. This highly developed solution offers many advantages but the main drawback continues to be its isolation from the university, which as a rule does not feel greatly committed.
– The creation of specific structures within the various teaching and research units (schools, departments, faculties). The limitation here is that these structures will only operate within their own academic field. Thus, Schools of Education will concern themselves with the continuing training of teachers, Schools of Agriculture will work on projects of assistance to agricultural communities, and so on.
– Another type of arrangement is the "consortium" linking one or more universities with the local/regional community. This arrangement makes it possible to broaden the approach to problems concerning one or more "local

community" and to ways of finding solutions. It also enables greater human and financial resources to be deployed.

The examples which follow give a clearer picture of the problems encountered in developing these various special bodies for university-community liaison, and their advantages and disadvantages.

1. SOME EXAMPLES OF LIAISON STRUCTURES IN TRAINING, RESEARCH AND PROBLEMS ANALYSIS

The following examples have been taken either from the preparatory papers of the February 1980 Conference, or from studies made for the meeting of the Institutional Management of Higher Education Programme (IMHE-CERI/OECD) for the discussion on "University consulting services: experiences and problems", (Paris, 21-22 April, 1980) [30].

a) **Liaison structures for the whole of the university**

This kind of arrangement can be illustrated by the following diagram which shows that the liaison structure (S_1) is shared by all the faculties or departments of the university, and can deal with research or teaching, or both.

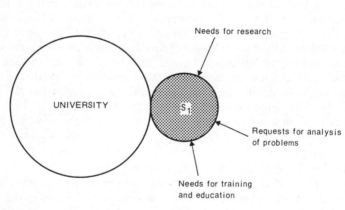

Obviously, the liaison structure (S_1) can be found in a great variety of institutional forms. For example, as regards *research,* even though the partner on the community side is usually a single body representing industrial enterprises, the structure can take a very wide variety of forms. These range from the organisation of specialised boards, services or secretariats responsible for co-ordinating research, developing outside contracts, selling patents or publishing findings, etc., to the establishment of companies or associations (sociétés) outside the university, generally non-profit-making, their earnings being paid to the parent university.

The liaison structures also differ as to aims and scope...

The Office of Research Administration of the University of Waterloo in Canada has for example the "prime responsibility for the furthering of research capability and productivity in the University. It is expected to inform faculty researchers of the research policies, goals and objectives of government agencies and of the major sectors of Canadian industry; to ensure that government and industrial leaders are aware of the research capabilities of the University; to assist in locating support for research in the form of grants and contracts; and to ensure that the University's policies and procedures will facilitate research contracts or grants between the University and any client or granting agency."

E.L. Holmes points out further that the Office is made up of a number of units with separately defined responsibilities:

- the Grant Section, which assists researchers in seeking grants for research and in preparing applications. In 1978-79, research grants to Waterloo faculty and staff totalled more than $6 m;
- Research contracts, which totalled $2.5 million in 1978 and 1979;
- the Inventor's Assistance Program: this original device, set up in 1976 and funded by the Government of Canada through a federally-owned corporation, Canadian Patents and Development Limited, evaluates inventions or discoveries submitted by persons within or outside the University. Evaluations, which cost $50, are done by appropriate experts at the University or elsewhere who provide assessments and recommendations on patent action or further development to the inventors. The inventor's information is held in strict confidence; the inventor retains rights to the invention. To June 1979, more than 500 inventions have been evaluated; some with market potential will be developed further through the Ontario Industrial Innovation Centre;
- the Centre for Process Development, established in 1978 to assist in the development and exploitation of new and improved chemical, biological or metallurgical processes at the pilot-plan level. To be selected for development in the Centre, a process must work on a bench scale, and must have a commercial patent. The Centre, although wholly owned by the University, functions as a semi-autonomous unit with its own Board of Directors. The Canadian Government's Department of Industry, Trade and Commerce is committed to provide $1 m over a period of five years to assist in the operation of the Centre;
- the Ontario Industrial Innovation Center is the newest unit. Its aim is to encourage the emergence of new ideas, to advise small and medium-sized enterprises in the development and manufacture of inventions, to help inventors and enterprises to use all the existing research and development resources;
- Finally, the Office is also responsible for ensuring that research involving human subjects is carried out in accordance with a strict code of ethics: all proposed research must be approved by the Office before the research can be undertaken.

The University of Waterloo, which was founded in 1957 and has 14 000 full-time students and 5 000 part-time students has thus set up, for research questions, an original type of body for liaison with the community. The various units comprising this body involve industrial firms and the Canadian Government. It should also be noted that the University of Waterloo is also associated with two Toronto firms in a "consortium". This consortium has for example negotiated a contract with the Canadian Government for the study and exploitation of solar energy.

Such a high degree of co-ordination of actions within the university means that the objectives and the role of research must be clearly defined by teaching staff, research workers and students. B.C. Matthews, Chairman and Vice Chancellor of the University said in 1978: "universities must play a new role in the application of new knowledge... opportunities for direct service by universities to industry, and society in general, have never been more evident. By becoming more directly involved with industry and government in research and technology transfer, and by offering assistance and education for entrepreneurs, a university can provide a new service as well as enrich its traditional functions."

There are also bodies which were set up by universities but have subsequently become financially and administratively independent. Associations and companies have thus been set up to tighten the links between university research and industry. They generally have the status of non-profit-making associations.

For example, the LR & D (*Leuven Research and Development Association*) (Société) in Belgium was set up in 1972 by the members of the Board of Trustees of the University of Leuven (Belgium) as a non-profit organisation. J. Bouchaert describes its aims as follows:

On the one hand, to establish a professional and commercial service organisation to handle development contracts, protect research results by applying for patents, ensure the industrial and commercial utilisation of technologies and know-how developed at the university laboratories through direct sales, conclude licence arrangements and participate in new industrial initiatives based upon these technologies and know-how. And on the other hand, to enable the scientific community to contribute to industrial innovation and to the socio-economic progress of our society.

LR & D is thus a commercial company in the services sector. Since it is non-profit-making, its earnings are reinvested in research activities at the university – itself by definition a non-profit-making establishment. The company's management strongly believes that a commercial approach is a very important factor in the business of technology transfer and that one of the criteria for measuring the effectiveness of university research results and developments in terms of their impact on industrial innovation is the price the market is willing to pay for such technologies and university know-how, and the costs involved in implementing these technologies and know-how or turning them into products to be sold on the marketplace.

Leuven Research and Development is legally and financially independent of the University, and operates under its own Articles of Association, General Meeting and Board of Directors. Its founders subscribed to the principle that a university should not be involved directly as an institution and take responsibility for activities which by definition have legal, financial and commercial implications. On the other hand, the Société is not allowed to establish its own facilities or institutes for applied and technological research alongside the university laboratories, nor does it intend to do so, apparently. The purpose of this type of service organisation is to perform a broker function and ensure the industrial and commercial exploitation of the techniques developed by the university and of the results of its research by establishing closer relations and concluding contracts with industry, government services and economic and social organisations. In doing this it does not interfere with the educational and research functions of the university, and has no voice in the definition of research policies, their orientation and priorities. Conversely, the university does not compel its teachers or the searchers in its laboratories to go through LR & D. The Société is not part of the university administration, but a body whose services the members of the university are entirely free to use or not. This position is based on its functional independence, which enables it to define its own objectives and line of conduct.

The relations of the Société with the university are governed by conventions which define the conditions under which the Société exercises its activities at the university. The following are some of the main clauses:

- For the use of the technic_
  equipment, computer time, e
  revenue as a fee to the uni_
  scientific personnel in LR
  week) of their time;
- Leuven Research and D
  and scientific personn_
- In practice, LR & F
  members are allow_
  remunerates them
  exceed 20 per ce
  reinvested in th
  that income;
- Leuven Res_
  personnel fo_
  technical activi_
  employees on the pa_
  authorities for their inform_
  salary scales, etc., must not b_
  sity.
- The Société submits its annual report and _
  the University for examination. The financia_
  independent auditor.

In 1979, LR & D's turnover amounted to US$1 200 000, an_
from contracts and licence agreements concluded with industry. The Soc_
cent of that income in fees to the University and retains 12 per cent of its gross _
to finance its activities. With this 12 per cent levy for overheads LR & D is comple_
self-supporting and has never received nor asked for any subsidy or funding. The 12 per
cent also covers its administrative costs, which are very small. The remainder of its
income (83 per cent) goes to finance the execution of development contracts in the
university's laboratories or is reinvested in those laboratories in case of profits.

The *North East London Polytechnic Company Limited* (NELPCO). This is a
United Kingdom case of a specific liaison structure between the North East London
Polytechnic and the community broadly defined. The objectives of the polytechnic in
setting it up were as follows:

- The need to create extra funds to increase the resources available to the
  polytechnic;
- The need to keep staff up-to-date with developments outside the polytechnic
  and thus provide opportunities for staff to develop into acknowledged
  authorities in their field;
- The need to provide staff with industrial/commercial experience where
  appropriate;
- The need to provide practical research applications as well as pure research
  opportunities;
- The need to provide facilities for students and staff to aid them in their teaching,
  research and consultancy work where such facilities cannot reasonably be
  provided from public funds;
- The need to "formalise" existing consultancy arrangements in the polytechnic,
  thus increasing;
- The opportunities for staff to widen their experience providing they have
  fulfilled their contractual obligations to the polytechnic;

...age and role of the polytechnic and enhance ...

... development of special courses.

...ove explicitly inspires almost all university-community ... to supplement the reduced resources granted to higher ...most all OECD countries. B. Littlewood points out in his ...or institution, a polytechnic is normally subject to financial ...ons prescribed by government legislation (e.g. the Education ...ment Act) and is subject to audit by a district auditor. Engaging ...es for the purpose of gain in fields which do not correspond closely ... of a polytechnic would normally be regarded as ultra vires. The ...nancial sanctions being imposed by the district auditor in the form of ...dividual officers is a very real one. It follows that if a polytechnic is to ...rovision of consulting, research and related activities on a commercial ...independently constituted limited liability company would seem to be the ...riate vehicle. This was the point of view adopted by NELP, although this ...ged it to find solutions to many questions of relationship with the company, ...interests and control.

...LPCO is registered under the U.K. Companies Act as a company limited by ...ntee. The company was created to provide consultancy and research services to ...ts, to engage in publishing, and to organise conferences, seminars and short courses ...specialised areas – all on a commercial basis. Whilst NELPCO is a separate legal ...ntity, it is closely associated with the North East London Polytechnic, drawing on the expertise and reputation of its teaching staff as well as its extensive physical resources.

NELPCO Ltd has been fully operational for a little more than twelve months. While it is yet early days in the life of the company, a number of interesting projects have already been undertaken and completed, and others are in hand. Contracts include:

- The design and building of specialist surveying equipment for use in Venezuela;
- Advice to a regional health authority in the United Kingdom on purchasing and contract procedure for pharmaceutical products;
- A computer programme for a sophisticated Management Business Game for a major United Kingdom industrial organisation;
- Purpose-designed post-graduate programme for building surveyors from Kenya;
- Specialist management development courses for an industrial corporation in the United Kingdom and also for the Retail Distribution Training Board;
- Advice to the Ministry of Education in Mexico on information systems for educational administration;
- The organisation of international conferences;
- The marketing and distribution of polytechnic publications.

To those in responsible positions in the NELPCO and the NELP, the advantages of this kind of structure are as follows:

- Many of the areas of activity outlined above are commercial or quasi-commercial by their very nature;
- NELPCO, as a commercial company, will be able to respond more flexibly to opportunities than is sometimes possible within the framework of a public sector educational institution;
- NELPCO will be able legally to engage in overtly commercial activities through agreements which might be a contravention of the Local Government Act if entered into by NELP;

- NELPCO provides a focus for approaches from client organisations and hence a source of contracts for faculties and/or individual staff;
- NELPCO ensures (via a Service Agreement with NELP) that NELPCO personnel may officially use NELP resources (its teaching staff, laboratory facilities, computer, office space, secretarial help, etc.) reimbursing NELP on an agreed basis;
- Given that NELP wishes to encourage research, consultancy, publication, updating of personal experience, etc., NELPCO can provide financial incentives in support of other non-financial incentives which already exist (e.g. keeping up-to-date, widening one's experience, producing new teaching material, becoming accepted as an expert in one's field, etc.);
- For NELP staff who are willing to spend time and energy over and above their contractual obligations to NELP, it will be possible, via NELPCO, to engage in additional activities (consultancy, summer schools, etc.) which bring direct financial reward rather than simply time off in lieu;
- As an educational institution the NELP may well enjoy the following indirect advantages:
    - more "expert" staff engaged in tackling real industrial problems;
    - more up-to-date teaching material; a greater output of research findings; increased viability via publications; greater educational impact via summer schools, and similar initiatives;
    - additional resources via NELPCO's disposable profits;
    - retention of staff who might otherwise be attracted to more lucrative jobs.

*
* *

The three examples given above describe joint liaison structures in the field of *research,* but in the field of *education and training* the universities have also gradually come to set up specific bodies for liaison with the community. This category includes the university "extension services" in the United Kingdom and the United States, and further education departments or "missions de formation permanente" in the French universities. In some cases "universities for the elderly" or "summer universities" could also be included, as well as other structures aiming at supplying educational services to groups that have hitherto been deprived of them.

For example, the *University of California Consortium for the Extended University,* United States [31] is a body founded by the Rector of the University in 1972. Its functions are as follows:
- To advise the President on university-wide policy affecting extended degree programmes;
- To facilitate the exchange of information throughout the University on extended degree programmes offered in California and elsewhere;
- To plan, develop and co-ordinate the use of various educational technology and media in the University's extended degree programmes;
- To engage in a continuous programme of research on the University's extended degree programmes, extended degree programmes elsewhere, non-traditional study, and the educational use of technology and media as they relate to extended degree programmes;

- To act as a university-wide contact for professional organisations, government agencies, regional and national associations, foundations and other parties interested in these programmes;
- To recommend to the President the establishment of off-campus learning centres;
- To encourage the campuses to develop extended degree programmes, to co-ordinate multi-campus programmes, and to encourage and authorise campuses to offer campus-based programmes on a state-wide basis;
- To design and develop degree programmes for part-time students in co-operation with the campuses:
  a) when such programmes promise greater cost effectiveness when offered by one or more campuses;
  b) when part-time students are unable because of distance or similar geographic constraints to enrol in a campus-based programme;
  c) when programmes are not otherwise offered by the campuses.

Another example is the *Faculty of Continuing Education* of the University of Montreal, Canada, which was set up in 1975 because of "the administrative paralysis of the Continuing Education Service. This paralysis was due to the number of bodies the Service had to deal with, to its lack of decision-making powers and to the increase in the volume of its activities." (G. Bourgeault, Colloque de l'AUPELF, 1979).

The Faculty of Continuing Education is a peripheral model, but in the long term the objective is that adult education should gradually be integrated into the normal structures of the University and that the latter should participate in an integrated scheme for continuing education. The Faculty has control over the programmes for adults at first-cycle level only. It has no professors and therefore has to take on professors or lecturers from the University or outside teachers. For everything else, its relations, jurisdiction and powers are the same as those of any other faculty. Compared with other teaching units, its characteristic lies in the potential student body it caters for, not in its disciplines or fields of study. It is also the only faculty with a research centre which carries out institutional research and more general research on education, in the light of the concepts of adult education.

The Faculty of Continuing Education has 12 000 students, and 600 teachers. The main areas to which it has addressed its services so far have been the following working sectors: the world of business, the world of communications, group activity organisers, nurses and teachers. The financing of the Faculty's activities follows the pattern in other universities in the Province of Quebec (academic fees and grants too are credited to educational institutions). Those responsible for this education-community liaison structure hope not only that the Faculty of Continuing Education will retain its links with the parent university, but that it will participate in the transformation of the university and of its social responsibility. "The future of adult education in the university and more particularly the future of the university in the context of continuing education is bound up with a radical transformation of the university... but this can only take place through the introduction of new types of solidarity. Traditionally, the university has been associated either with professional corporations or with people belonging to the so-called "upper" classes of society. Without a new type of institutional solidarity with other groups, the wished-for transformations have no future..."

b) **Second case: liaison structures attached to particular departments of the university, not to the university as a whole**

This type of liaison structure, S_2, attached to departments, faculties, schools or colleges of the university, can be represented by the following diagram:

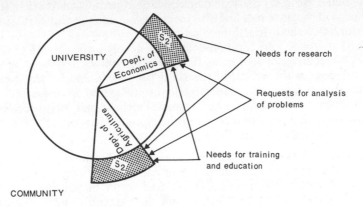

For example, two departments of the university may each set up liaison structures in their own field of competence: agriculture or economics. In practice this type of structure is more usual than the previous one, i.e. the single structure for the whole university. The reasons for this are generally the following:

- The initiatives of individuals or groups of research workers or academics are more easily taken into consideration in the various faculties, schools or departments, which provide a more flexible framework for negotiating with the community;
- Historically, some university faculties or departments have established fairly close connections with the community: e.g. faculties of medicine with the health care sector (even if action is confined to the university hospital); faculties of science with the research sector (relations with certain types of industry); etc.

On the other hand, some sectors of the university remain isolated, either because of the lines on which their teaching and research is organised, or because they are unwilling to enter into any commitments with the community, or because of an institutional inability to respond to the complex expectations and needs of the outside world.

The following few examples show the variety of relationships that can be worked out between individual departments of the university and the community. We shall, however, give rather less space to them than to liaison structures for the university as a whole, because individual departmental liaison structures are very widespread and take such a great variety of forms that no single one can be considered typical.

The Atatürk University (Turkey), for example, was founded in 1958, in the Eastern province of Erzurum, with the aim, to quote Hursit Ertugrul, of "actively contributing to the improvement of the social, economic and cultural life of the surrounding population". Since exchanges between the university and the region through informal contacts between individuals had not produced any significant or durable results, the following sectors of the university have developed their own institutional machinery:

- The Faculty of Letters has set up an ad hoc group to survey and conserve cultural practices which are in danger of dying out;
- The Faculty of Business Administration is developing "extended education" by organising training courses in accountancy and simple business management for large numbers of young people who do not belong to the University;

91

- The Department of Preventive Medicine, which is part of the Faculty of Medicine, is largely an "extended education" institution. It organises radio and television programmes, and also meetings outside the University to inform the community about health problems;
- The Faculty of Agriculture is even more deeply involved with the community. The whole series of continuing training programmes have been introduced and developed for the benefit of the rural population and for staffs employed by government agencies. Other agricultural extension projects are genuine examples of "service in action", especially those that give direct assistance to farmers with a view to increasing their productivity and therefore improving their standard of living.

The Vienna University of Agricultural Science and Technology (Austria) is another example. It is the only technical university in Austria where agriculture, forestry and timber management, cultivation techniques and water management, and food and fermentation technology can be studied from the biological and ecological points of view. A hundred and sixty professors, 170 other employees and 2 500 students work on these four groups of disciplines or study areas in the 30 research and teaching institutes of the University. Research and training in the four areas mentioned above also concern other aspects. energy, communications, town and country planning and the protection of the rural and natural environment, etc.

Because of the great variety of disciplines and subjects taught and researched in it, the University is popularly known as the "University of diversity". As the Conference of Austrian Rectors points out, the various institutes making up this highly centralised University have developed a whole series of liaison mechanisms with their partners in the community:

- With the Federal authorities: the Federal Ministry for Agriculture and Forestry, the Federal Ministry for Health and the Protection of the Environment, the Federal Ministry for Buildings and Technology, and the Federal Ministry for Science and Research;
- With the Public Associations representing the social and economic interests of the workers. The Chambers of Agriculture have a privileged position in this respect. The Chambers of Commerce, Chambers of Agricultural Employees and Chambers of Agriculture are ex officio members of the University;
- With the Private Associations, often on a tripartite basis, including the University, employers and trade unions;
- With the Academic Associations. Nearly all of the thirty Institutes have links with these Associations, of which they are sometimes members (e.g. the Zoological and Botanical Associations, the Austrian Association of Jurists for Agricultural Questions, etc.).

Lastly, it is important to stress the particularly close relations which have been established with the media. Many of the Institutes' special services also supply information to people working in the various sectors of agriculture and forestry. The University has its own publication – Die Bodenkultur – named after the University itself, and also produces about 30 periodicals of varying quality. This is convincing evidence of the importance this University – and more generally, all Austrian universities – attach to the need to supply the community with information.

c) **Third case: Consortia linking one or more universities with the community**

The differences between this type of university-community liaison structure and the two preceding types can be illustrated by the following diagram:

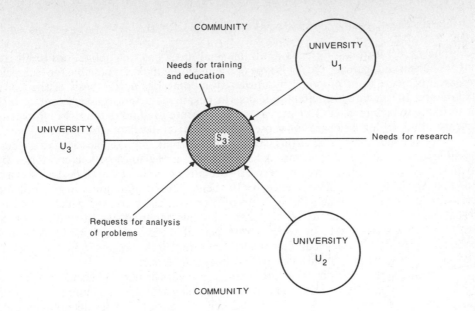

These structures have the following characteristics:

— They have been created to contribute to the analysis of problems, and to the promotion of solution in the fields of industry and the economic and social development of the towns or regions in which they have been set up;
— They enjoy considerable administrative autonomy, and are financed by the community partners, with whom they have equal representation – all of which lends a certain "neutrality" to these mechanisms;
— They generally link several universities to various local or regional groups and enterprises.

The following examples, like those given for the preceding cases, reflect the compositional and organisational variety of these structures.

The National Inter-University Institute for Silicates, Soils and Materials (INISMa), Mons, Belgium, was founded in 1973 in the form of a non-profit-making association, by four institutions working together:

— The State University, Mons, an autonomous university institution;
— The Polytechnic Faculty of Mons, an autonomous university institution;
— The National University of Silicates, founded in 1938 on the initiative of the Polytechnic Faculty of Mons and 22 companies representing the main Belgian ceramics and pottery firms at that time;
— The Inter-Commune Association for the Economic and Regional Development of the Centre Regions and the Borinage area.

This Consortium, set up by the joint efforts of the public authorities, industrial circles and the universities, deliberately chose to confine its activities to the following areas: materials, recycling of industrial waste and by-products, energy conservation, solar energy, the exploitation of mineral wealth and industrial pollution.

The Directorate of the Institute centralises all applications from industry for research or testing. It contacts whatever university services might in principle take part in the research. If necessary, it organises the appropriate technical discussions and supplies any additional staff or equipment required. It co-ordinates the research on lines which ensure that when the study is completed the manufacturer concerned receives a combined report, each professor being responsible for the part that he has dealt with.

The Directorate also attends to all financial questions, the obligations of all the parties concerned, patents, etc. This type of organisation makes it possible for technical research projects to be proposed by university laboratories on the basis of their own experience. In this case, the Directorate does its best to make the necessary contact with firms likely to be interested. In some cases, the Institute itself takes the risk of financing research and selling a licence for subsequent industrial development.

R.E. Baland points out that this liaison structure makes it possible to make the best possible use of the resources and skills available in the university laboratories by fostering close co-operation among services specialising in the research design of work, and tests in the field of applied science, for the benefit of the community in general, and industry in particular. When the scale and urgency of the problems which are to be researched exceed the capacity of the universities' own facilities, the Institute is able to put research workers and laboratories at the disposal of the professors in charge, and if necessary provide additional equipment and apparatus for the university laboratories. It can, in fact, use its own infrastructure and financial resources.

Working in the other direction, the Institute provides firms with specialists who can not only visit factories to locate and discuss problems before beginning a research assignment or a series of trials, but can also help to translate the results obtained into practice. It also attends to the market surveys which necessarily precede all technological research for the manufacturing and marketing of a product. Finally, the continuing dialogue with industry is institutionalised by the active participation on the governing board of the Institute of leading industrialists and representatives of the public authorities.

According to R.E. Baland, one of the reasons why the Institute has been so successful is that it limits the area of its activities. Its efficiency is due to a careful selection of specific disciplines which its member bodies are well equipped to handle and in which they are determined to remain among the leaders. The university laboratories which are members of the INISMa are not of course all concerned with the same discipline, but they are interested in the same research subjects, though from different points of view. For example, in the science of materials, this concept of co-ordinated technological research makes it easier for a solid-state physicist, a synthesis chemist, a heat engineer, a physico-chemist specialising in chemical kinetics and a cristallographer to work in the same team.

The University-City Science Center (UCSC), Philadelphia, United States is another example of a liaison structure with an interesting history and development.

In the early 1960s, an informal group of Philadelphian businessmen, university and government officials who were particularly aware of the problems of urban blight, unemployment and a declining tax base to support a growing need for essential services in the cities, decided to develop a coherent plan of action to overcome these difficulties. Each had his own objectives in mind. Those from the universities wanted a mechanism that would facilitate application of faculty experience and knowledge to the solution of complex problems facing the cities. They also wanted to find ways to share costly facilities, and to create a common centre for continuing education programmes for adults. The city, through its agencies, was becoming desperate over the erosion of the tax base, the flight of jobs to the suburbs and the general need for urban revitalisation. The Federal Government, through both direct and indirect action programmes, was committed to reverse the trend towards urban decay, improve the availability of housing, open up jobs on a more equitable basis for minorities, many of whom were concentrated in the city.

After defining common objectives, this informal group set up a private non-profit-making institution, under the laws of the State of Pennsylvania, whose

29 universities, colleges and medical schools took up all the shares, against a minimum contribution of $10 000 each. This was supplemented by outright cash grants, aggregating $156 000, from local industry and business. Total paid-in working capital from both sources over a six-year period amounted to $648 000. The University-City Science Center was incorporated in 1963 and began operations early in 1964, the municipal authorities having placed 19 acres of land in the centre of the town at the disposal of the Center.

"The Science Center is engaged in the application with member institutions or Resident Organisations:

- As a permanent residence for private companies and coporations as well as non-profit technical organisations who see an advantage to the Science Center's convenient location and productive environment;
- As a data management organisation capable of designing, organising and operating data management systems;
- As a catalyst for inter-institutional co-operation;
- As a non-profit umbrella, partner, financial manager in grant applications or solicitation of government contract;
- As a home for experimental projects needing office or laboratory space;
- As a service organisation, providing a variety of management and consultative services;
- As a training organisation in any of its fields of expertise.

The Center has expanded considerably. Its annual operational budget is now almost $7 million (spent by the 75 Research Centres). The City of Philadelphia, the Federal Government and the universities all seem to have benefited from this original structure founded on credibility, objectivity and neutrality.

Another example, again from the United States, is the *City-University Consortium of Detroit*, set up in 1976 by the City of Detroit (1 500 000 inhabitants of which 50 per cent blacks, main centre of the US automobile industry with a long history of trade unionism) and Wayne State University (35 000 students) on the basis of a grant from the National Science Foundation, and with the object of participating in the analysis of urban problems and finding solutions which make full use of the existing resources of the university and the city. The university had already in the past made in-depth studies of the city's problems, and trained a large proportion of its officials. Relationships were then on an individual level. With the rapid growth of the city and the university, the desire of both sides to co-operate led to the setting up of this consortium. The Consortial Steering Committee which runs this liaison structure is made up of five persons nominated by the city – three of them from the Mayor's office, one from the Planning Department and one from the Training Department, and five nominees from the university – one from the office of the Vice-President for Urban Affairs, two from the Center of Urban Studies, one from the Urban Studies Module of the University Studies Weekend College, and one from the Community Services Division.

The Consortium has an annual budget of $66 500. The Consortium Steering Committee meets regularly to allocate this sum among the various projects. The financing system is flexible: if new projects are submitted which would not be covered by this annual local amount, additional funds can be freed depending on the quality and effectiveness of the results of projects foreseen in the programme. The university and the town are the sole judges of this systematic assessment of projects. Furthermore, the human and material resources of the two partners are fully used for the implementation of projects.

According to O. Feinstein, the Consortium has two functions: a service function and a co-operation function. The first ensures rapid responses by the university to the requests for services from the city; the second makes it possible to deal with problems of common interest to the town and the university. Since the Consortium brings about a veritable osmosis between the city and the university, the latter is induced to review certain aspects of its training and research programmes. The interaction of the service function with the teaching and research functions thus reflects the consistency of the university's involvement in the city's problems "... without either partner losing its integrity".

The Planning and Research Bureau for the Development of Co-operation in the Agricultural and Food Industries in Southern France (referred to below as the "Bureau Méridional") has a structure which is quite different from those of the examples given above. It is made up of agricultural co-operatives of the Regional Council and the University of Aix-Marseille II. Its task is to prepare, present and manage the programme for promoting agriculture through co-operation, and "to consider all activities likely to promote the agriculture and food sector, particularly through the development of co-operation, and to study all proposals in this respect put forward by public or private bodies, whether national, regional or local". This type of body is particularly important in the context of present-day French regionalisation. It constitutes in fact an intermediary body for the implementation of the policies of the regional public authorities, since under the 1972 Law the latter are not authorised to act directly.

The representatives of the University, who are members of the General Assembly, the governing board and the Directorate of the Bureau Méridional, are economists and geographers. The University's contribution to this body is mainly one of research. Carried out by a team of economic, statistical and agricultural experts, this research helps the Bureau Méridional by using a simulation model of the region's agriculture to evaluate the implications of decisions likely to affect agricultural development. The team is financed by an annual grant from the Bureau Méridional to its research departments, while the Bureau itself is financed by a grant from the regional authorities.

The most remarkable achievement of this liaison structure was the elaboration, by the Bureau Méridional and with the help of the team from the Faculty, of a five-year plan for the protection of Provençal agriculture. This plan was adopted by the regional authorities and provided with an exceptional appropriation of 150 million francs covering a period of five years. During this period the team will keep a close watch on the implementation of the objectives. The plan provides for a number of measures aimed at preserving agriculture activities which are not only seriously threatened by international trade, but adversely affected in many ways by local land uses.

We conclude this review of various types of joint liaison structures by mentioning the "continuing education consortia" which, in France, for example, are spreading rapidly.

Thus, in Grenoble, the CUIDEP (University Information, Research and Documentation Centre for Continuing Education) was set up by the city's three universities and by the National Polytechnic Institute of Grenoble. Its objective is to alert the working population to the opportunities for continuing education, to assist those concerned in this training (private or public training bodies, trade unions, firms) and to inform both sides about entitlement to training and available courses. This multidisciplinary centre is therefore an inter-university body. It is at the disposal of all local communities (trade unions, works councils, in-firm training services, associations, joint representation committees, local authorities, public establishments, etc.), informing and advising them and organising training sessions or information meetings at their request. It has its own staff and issues an information bulletin.

With rather different aims, the universities in the Lille region – a particularly important economic and urban area – have also joined forces to set up a University Centre for Continuing Education which co-operates in launching "collective activities" related to the industrial crisis in this previously highly developed area which has now been affected by the crisis which has hit the older forms particularly hard.

In both cases, it is not merely a question of extending traditional educational activities to adults, but of introducing new kinds of training, including "lower level" training, in close co-operation with all the local authorities.

2. COMMON PROBLEMS IN THE DEVELOPMENT OF THESE LIAISON STRUCTURES

The examples given above illustrate three types of special university-community liaison structures: those common to the whole university (S_1); those attached to particular departments, faculties or schools of the university (S_2); and consortia linking one or more universities with the community (S_3).

This classification should not be allowed to conceal the complexity and variety of the "institutionalised" relationships which some universities have with the community, i.e. with a great variety of different kinds of groups. Furthermore, many universities which are deliberately involved in activities with the community combine these three types of structure, which are not mutually exclusive. However, the cases given above, together with others brought to our notice, reveal certain problems and tendencies in the development of liaison structures.

a) **Common problems**

   i) *Difficulties inherent in "partnership"*

Abandoning one's own lonely furrow, getting a dialogue going and working with partners with whom one is generally unfamiliar, means for both sides:

- *Conflicts of interest and a certain loss of independence*
  Thus, relations between the North-East London Polytechnic and the North-East London Polytechnic Company Ltd had to be worked out with particular care so as to avoid such conflicts of interest. The NELPCO negotiated an agreement with the NELP for the joint use of their services. This agreement clearly defines the conditions under which the Company may use polytechnic staff, facilities and material, and vice versa;
- *The sharing of authority and information*
  The fact that initiative, financing and resources are a matter either for the institution of higher education or for the community involves a problem with regard to the allocation of authority and the diffusion of information. The proposition that there should be a variety of institutional structures should not be taken as implying that the complexity of the two partners can be forgotten, and particularly the fact that the community is constantly subject to conflicts. It would be illusory to deny the existence of these conflicts and to claim that any development in the relations between higher education and the community would not run counter to the independence of the former. In the final analysis, all choices and policies depend on the way in which the various forces involved are represented in the co-operative bodies.
- *Reconsidering accepted forms of language, knowledge and the approach to the problem* (Cf. Part One, Chapter 2)
  The university remains speculative, theoretical and abstract, whilst the surrounding community is practical, concrete and concerned with achieving a

97

number of short-term projects, as L.M. Hill of the University of California at Irvine (United States) has pointed out. Negotiating and working with the community means that esoteric language has to be modified, specialised knowledge relativised and empirical knowledge rehabilitated.

– *A change in the behaviour of the partners to one another*
As the University of Aix-Marseille II points out, "a far from negligible number of local and regional elected representatives consider contracts providing financial backing for co-operation to be mere capital grants, do not read the report submitted to them and resent being advised by academics... ".

ii) Difficulties arising from structural differences between the partners

"If industry and the university often find it difficult to understand one another, this is because their internal structures are radically different, even opposed. The university is organised essentially in disciplines: physics, chemistry, etc., while industry is organised by production sectors: shipbuilding, aeronautics, etc. There is at present no branch of industry that does not need all disciplines, and there is no discipline that cannot be useful to all branches of industry. In some business circles there is still the illusion that in developing science and engineering one will somehow develop engineering industries. But the latter need chemistry, data processing and sociology just as much as they need mechanical engineering," says G. Denielou in his report to the Conference. This discrepancy between community structures and requirements and the structures of the university concerns not only the economic and industrial sector and applied research, but also training and education. The University of British Columbia, Canada, describing its Continuing Education Centre, considers that differences of opinion concerning basic education constitute the greatest challenge: "the academic departments and many individual faculties quite naturally view general education from the perspective of their own academic discipline. The adults in the community, on the other hand, quite naturally look towards the problems they and society face in daily life. Such problems usually cannot easily be solved with expertise applied from one academic discipline but rather require an interdisciplinary or cross-disciplinary approach". Many other examples could be given from the information available. This interdisciplinary and inter-professional problem is constantly mentioned by the universities. We have therefore devoted the second chapter of Part Three to this question.

iii) Difficulties related to the status, rewards and remuneration of staff working in these liaison structures

Generally speaking, when the university does not concern itself with community problems as a deliberate policy, the activities organised by the liaison bodies for the benefit of the community have little prestige because of their practical and short-term slant. To be engaged in activities of a lower caste than conventional teaching and research means losing status in the eyes of one's colleagues. As E.W. Weidner, Chancellor of the University of the University of Wisconsin-Green Bay says, "in American higher education, there has been too much separatism. There has been too much isolation of extension activities. Historically, the Land Grant Colleges embraced the idea of a social mission but too often the majority of professors have preferred to see that mission performed through the mechanism of an extension service which is at the bottom of the prestige ladder and confined in scope and subject areas."

Over and above the question of status, it is the problem of the system of rewards and promotion that faces practically all universities working for the community. The system of promotion is generally based on teaching and research activities of the monodisciplinary type or at least on the traditional organisation of knowledge. It is therefore difficult for any teaching or research activity that does not coincide with this organisation to be taken into account in individual career development.

The document from Miami University, Oxford, Ohio, United States, for example, states: "Generally, universities are heavily discipline-oriented with the reward system geared to specialisation and basic research publication... in spite of the strengthening of the linkage between the communities and higher education and increased attention to problem-focussed activities by the universities, the traditional reward systems for the universities persist with incentives to stimulate higher-level specialisation and scholarly publication. For example, in spite of the increased demand for problem-focussed education, present reward systems do not encourage, rather they are a deterrent to, such education. The most significant contribution of the OECD Report could well be a forceful urging of an alteration of reward systems in the universities to provide incentives for problem-focussed educational research and service and for interaction with the community at the same level as those now provided for scholarly research and publication. It is our firm conviction that such a change in reward systems would inject more university expertise into the consideration of today's complex problems... to the great benefit of society and the universities".

Lastly, questions of pay and job security are very often raised. Activities benefiting the community bring neither permanent appointments nor higher pay. On the contrary, insofar as these activities interfere with teaching and research work, they hobble the careers of teaching staff. A few universities are trying to find a solution to this problem. The University of Western Michigan (United States) was given the following recommendation by its Community Services Committee: At the departmental level, operationalise a clear and objective formula detailing the actual weights to be given to various faculty activities when decisions are made in reference to:

> *i)* promotion,
> *ii)* salary, and
> *iii)* tenure.

Such a formula would be fleshed out with actual activity descriptions and weights by each department or institute at the university.

These questions of status, rewards, pay and job security are all the more relevant in that it is difficult to find talented academics with a sufficient understanding of community problems. "Often potentially good consultants are also the most able in a teaching capacity; an attendant risk is that they may become over-extended or perhaps diverted from their normal responsibilities. How best can we develop consulting skills in academic staff?" This point made by NELPCO tallies with a remark made at the University of Rouen (France) to the effect that "university research workers and technical staff cannot be asked to carry out basic research and applied research and development all at the same time".

Some system must therefore be found to enable these liaison structures to be run by qualified staff which implies, first of all, the finding of urgent solutions to the above problems.

iv) *The precarious position of the community liaison structure*

Since they break with university tradition, such structures may arouse opposition not only from the majority of the teaching body but also from certain "regular" students (quite apart from their possible opposition to certain activities because of their nature, as the University of California points out with regard to research for military purposes). Representatives of the community, too, sometimes voice their fears, examples being the economic competition that certain applied research services may present, interference in their "private affairs", etc.

Finding themselves in this precarious situation, certain bodies tend to strengthen their position:

- By mounting publicity campaigns to make the services they offer better known: "the University has itself to present its activities and achievements to the general public and to the users of research services": statement by Tampere University of Technology, Finland. The Technical University of Denmark takes the same view;
- By increasing their authority vis-à-vis the parent university. The Industrial Innovation Centre of the University of Waterloo, Canada, for example, "must have the authority to make decisions and negotiate contracts on behalf of the University..."; or
- By obtaining its own sources of finance which – in some cases – may be considerable: the University of Wisconsin-Madison (United States) has founded the Wisconsin Alumni Research Foundation empowered to receive "income which supports research and contributes to the construction of new campus buildings and research facilities".

v) *An institutional momentum that may lead to the increasing isolation of the liaison body*

It has already been pointed out that some teaching or research bodies have had difficulty in asserting themselves and remain marginal or even cease to exist. When the machinery works well, the body clearly becomes more and more independent in terms of finance and staffing and may even achieve physical independence, obtaining new premises. This is always related to an increasing level of self-financing and this in turn leads to a new appraisal of the relations that exist between the university and the community. A significant example here is the Metallurgical Research Centre (CRM) of the University of Liège (Belgium). This Centre is not new, since it was founded in 1948. Several aspects of its organisation and even its name have been changed several times since then but it has not changed its position with regard to the University or its original social objective: research to improve metallurgical manufacturing processes and product quality. The large amount of work done by the Centre is clear from its annual budget of about B.Frs.400 million and its staff of over 300 people, including 90 graduates – most of them civil engineers. The vigour of the Centre also seems to have been reinforced by the fact of having its own staff, employed under contracts that are different from – and may appear in many ways to be more favourable than – those of the University staff. Through its connections with the academic world and its familiarity with the main trends of international research, the Centre is able to rise above the immediate concerns that threaten to dominate the industrial world voiced variously by management, unions or possibly authorities, i.e. profitability questions, job security, hammering out a compromise between diverging stances, etc.

Because of its intermediary position, the Centre can also stimulate and facilitate exchanges between the University and the community. It gives strictly academic bodies a better insight into industrial realities and the ways in which their work can be geared to those realities. It induces business leaders to recognise the value of the research, even the fundamental research, undertaken in the University's laboratories. The Centre's position may also lead it to negotiate with whatever bodies it feels are best qualified in the University of Liège and other universities as the case may be.

In spite of the links described, the Metallurgical Research Centre remains basically independent of the University. P. Minon has misgivings on this point. "The Centre's independence with regard to the University is so marked that it may be wondered whether the University is still in touch with the community through the Centre. Such cases reveal how imprecise the boundaries are between university activities conducted in co-operation with the community and scientific activities already initiated by the community... The case of the CRM leads one to wonder why an institution of this nature

100

is anxious to remain so independent of a university to which it is nevertheless so close."

Lastly, the transformation of a part of the university into a productive and competitive sector of the economy. In some countries this is not a new phenomenon. In others this new development of "selling" services is not only a function of closer ties with the community (and not necessarily just with industry) but also a function of the need to survive the current financial crisis in higher education. The selling of services, however, produces a whole series of problems, the first of which naturally affects the very goals of the university. They include:

- The risk of major imbalances between certain faculties or departments: for example, the vast market in continuing education may produce revenues giving some of them unacceptable power. On the other side of the coin, Tampere University of Technology (Finland) reports that "next year the University will be able to use the funds obtained from service research for practically any of its activities";
- The risk of causing conflict by selling services at non-competitive prices: the University of Strathclyde (United Kingdom) points out that its programme offers "normal architectural services at standard fees"; A.M. Israelsson says that "scientists at the University of Luleå, Sweden, may not enter into competition with consultancy firms in the various sectors of activity";
- The risk of university resources being exploited for commercial purposes without due return: J. Moe and K. Stenstadvold described the example of SINTEF, an independent foundation attached to the Norwegian Institute of Technology (NTH), the only university-level technical establishment in Norway. Its setting up, in 1950, was strongly supported by the industrial and commercial world. SINTEF has a twofold mission: firstly to stimulate applied research and development work in the NTH so that this can also be of benefit to educational activity there, and secondly, through its research and consultancy activities on behalf of industrial and commercial firms and the public services, to contribute to the research and development work the country needs particularly in the technological field. At the end of 1979 the number of full-time staff at SINTEF was 880. Running expenses, equivalent therefore to its operating budget, totalled about 151 million kroner. "The salient feature of SINTEF, perhaps, is the virtual absence of formal and written rules and agreements in its relations with the NTH. Broadly speaking a common understanding of the need for co-operation has been successfully created, not forgetting that for constant adjustment to the changing internal and external conditions. Even so, some questions could have given rise to friction or difficulty, such as: to what extent can and should SINTEF market under its name the skills that are brought together by virtue of this co-operation; how can NTH avoid being overshadowed by its very large and vigorous off-spring?"

A last example is the Massachusetts Institute of Technology (MIT), United States, which has always had close contacts with industry and notes that "the fundamental difference between the objectives of the academy and industry requires substantial sensitivity to their respective concerns and a continuing review of the problems to ensure that the outcome of this relationship is a happy one for all parties". O.R. Simha quotes the following particular examples of issues arising in its relations with industry:

- Proprietary rights in research results: to deal with this question MIT maintains standard contractual procedures for patents, copyrights, and licensing agreements;

- Disclosure of findings: MIT maintains the right to disclose the products of its research without exception;
- Conflicts of interest: MIT has set up a special review and evaluation procedure to ensure that faculty and staff do not find themselves in compromising situations, the basic principle being that their first loyalty is to MIT;
- Finance and administration: all contractual and financial issues are the responsibility of the Office of Sponsored Programmes, the staff of which deals with and supervises all business aspects of MIT's research programmes.

b) Trend towards a single university-community liaison system

Observation and analysis of the various university-community liaison structures show that there is a distinct tendency towards the *development of a kind of liaison "system" in which there are a variety of institutional structures, common to the whole university.* Indeed, both partners are so complex and so varied that it would be an illusion to hope that any single, rigid institutional "structure" involving the whole university and the whole community could function efficiently. Certain sectors of the university develop relations with certain elements in the community. For this reason it seems better to use the term *"liaison system"* which is flexible and allows for individual and collective initiatives on either side, promoting activities in educational and research fields to benefit the community and thus promote the recurrent relationship of these two functions and not their separation.

Some universities are moving in this direction. They have combined the three structures (S_1, S_2 and S_3) previously analysed, at the same time leaving room for the setting up of informal groups to develop certain projects, the whole being harmonized in a flexible and coherent system where neither the co-ordination of activities nor the dissemination of information are organised on mandatory lines. G. Denielou stresses the importance of this plurality: "institutional mechanisms for promoting flows and exchanges between the university and community cannot be simple. Let there be no illusions about this. Nothing will be improved just by seting up a liaison committee between the university and industry. The links must be numerous and complex, numerous so as personally to affect every member of the university, and complex because they must reach out into a great many different areas. The university and the community cannot be treated as two mechanical parts to be linked by a connecting rod or tube. The grafting together of their respective tissues also implies social and even family relationships. The applicable metaphor is biological. We must be on our guard against the illusion of simplistic solutions. The problem can only be solved if seen in its full complexity".

The two main reasons given by universities for developing this liaison "system" are these.

First, the better continuity and co-ordination of the activities promoted by the various university faculties or institutes. The Austrian Rectors' Conference reports that the wide range of links maintained by the 30 institutes of the Agricultural University of Vienna "encourage centrifugal tendencies making the integration of the university more difficult". The University of Dijon, France, also points out that the faculties' direct relations with the outside world have led to the creation of often informal ad hoc committees which "end up by developing their own specificity and becoming more or less merged, on the university side, with one or more laboratories, so that the definition of their objectives falls largely outside the university Council". The University of Rouen, France, in addition to the liaison bodies it has set up in other fields (research), has deliberately instituted a "University Continuing Education Service" covering all the teaching and research units (UER) and university technological institutes (IUT). 'This system is highly appreciated by industry which no longer has to apply to several different organisations to arrange further training for employees."

The need for this kind of co-ordinating system is keenly felt by some of our correspondents. N. Iceton of the University of New England in Australia, for example, remarks that by the end of 1979 the University of New England had a whole series of community liaison bodies. There is, however, very little liaison between them, so that there can be no joint planning and little shared knowledge of the activities carried out. "It is clear that all the agencies face some common problems, or will do so in due course. Yet they are not well informed about each other, and their activities neither emerge from any overall UNE policy that defines their scope, nor do they express any ongoing policy line after they emerge: no benefits of synergy are made to flow from these activities as a whole. There is no machinery through which these developments were or are facilitated on a routine basis. Within their own fields, each operates out of a "small-farmer" mentality. This means that while things go well, they tend to be preoccupied with the day-to-day work and lack long-term foresight. When difficulties arise they are taken by surprise and have no contingency plans or support network ready to pull the necessary strings. In fact this characterises the overall institutional approach up to the present time. Only a minority of entrepreneurs operate out of "big picture" foresight and they do so solely on an individual basis which has no effect at institutional level".

Second, response to the community's pluridisciplinary needs. As was stressed at the opening of this chapter, bodies attached to the various faculties and departments usually deal with specific problems: departments of education handle continuing education for teachers, departments of agriculture work with agricultural groups, and so on. As a solution to this problem, the Atatürk University in Turkey has set up a Public Relations Office responsible for co-ordinating the various activities undertaken by the different university colleges "because of the interdisciplinary nature of the work carried out for the community".

This vital problem of the inter- and pluridisciplinary nature of the community's needs is taken up again in Part Three of this report.

CONCLUSION

A first comment here, therefore, concerns the diversity of university-community liaison structures. Highly varied, they depend on the different higher education systems in each country, the nature of the partners involved, their degree of independence and the objectives pursued, but they also depend on the people concerned and on a large number of factors related to the prevailing situation. None of the three models we have described seems to qualify for any kind of precedence. The most that can be done is to identify the specific difficulties in each case or the varyingly long-term risks and rigidities.

Another important factor seems to us to be the assessment of the medium or long-term effects of these developments on the internal functioning of the universities or, in other words, the innovation potential that these new structures represent for the system as a whole. In general terms, whilst attention must be drawn to the efforts made by certain universities to establish relations with various groups in the community, and the positive measures introduced by certain governments (United Kingdom, France, Canada, United States, Sweden, etc.), there should be no illusions about the effect that this type of innovation can have on the objectives and functioning of the university.

Most of the experiments described not only failed to involve all activities in the universities concerned, they also arouse strong opposition from the more traditional sectors of the university and sometimes of the community. Furthermore, every time a project has gone on long enough to enable the long-term trend to be analysed, negative aspects can be detected which greatly reduce the ultimate effect of these changes.

In this connection, four main mechanisms may be said to be protecting the universities from the disruption that involvement in the social, cultural and economic environment might trigger off:

- The establishment within the university of an ad hoc structure of these relations, with its own staff, budget and administration, protecting the static character of the university as a whole for the alleged reason of enhancing independence and scientific objectivity;
- Many "window-dressing" exercises, in which a number of programmes create an artificial commotion around impervious cores;
- The overall marginalisation process involving persons or structures which, while keeping the experiments under way, diminishes their effects and significance throughout higher education and within each institution;
- "Institutional migration" which, by giving birth to new and independent bodies, meets the immediate demand for effectiveness, but in reality removes the risk of full-scale change.

The desire for a simple kind of institutional solution paradoxically entails the risk of gradually marginalising university-community relations. The reason is that once it is identified and brought together in a unified institutional framework, what amounts to a source of unwanted innovation can easily be pushed to one side. Everything that fails to comply with the model aimed at or is difficult to fit into bureaucratic norms runs the risk of gradual elimination by the institution to become an outlying activity – even, and perhaps particularly, if it represents an important aspect of social reality. It is therefore important to be very cautious in assessing the true significance of this tendency to set up individualised community relation systems and to bear in mind that their success and the independence they acquire, even if easy to justify pragmatically, may be perceived in contradictory ways. The universities would be well advised to regard these numerous liaison strategies simply as a temporary phase, corresponding to the need to create clearly identifiable decision-making bodies and pressure groups capable of influencing the whole of the university institution at a later stage and therefore to be gradually phased out as separate institutions.

Chapter 3

INITIATIVE FOR, AND FINANCING OF, ACTIVITIES TO BENEFIT THE COMMUNITY

For a better grasp of the dynamics of university-community relations, we have to understand how these relations are established, who requires them, who is at their origin or brings them into being, and how much of their financial and human resources local and national authorities are prepared to invest in developing them. Initiative and financing – the terms are closely linked – are considered here as a whole, but specific case studies would obviously be necessary to follow the route taken by proposals and decisions – although most of the time even the people involved do not themselves know exactly what that route is.

1. WHO TAKES THE INITIATIVE?

The survey that was carried out endeavoured to discover the origin of the activities developed for the benefit of the community by suggesting three main possibilities on their own or in combination, namely higher educational institutions (and in this case, which group: teachers, students, members of the governing board?), local/regional communities (appointed or elected bodies, firms, associations, interest groups, trade unions, and even spontaneous unorthodox groupings set up for the need of the moment) or centralised or national bodies (or in some cases international organisations).

This question was answered by 119 higher educational institutions in 22 Member countries (71 universities and 48 schools or post-secondary institutes) which listed 180 activities originating as follows:

- 94 activities, or about 52.5 per cent arose out of an initiative of a higher educational institution,
- 42 activities, 23.5 per cent, arose out of an initiative taken by local/regional communities,
- 29 activities, 16 per cent, arose out of an initiative taken at central or national level and
- 15 activities, about 8 per cent, arose out of an initiative at higher educational level taken jointly with other local/regional/national community bodies.

In the main, therefore, the initiative lies with the university (over 50 per cent, plus 8 per cent for activities of joint origin). This could be interpreted in several ways (outgoing attitude on the part of the university, the search for new financial resources, pressure from certain teachers or students, etc.), but it is apparently considered in certain countries that the university itself has to take the first step in breaking out of the isolation it has sometimes deliberately chosen. The survey carried out in France by Y. Laplume for the February 80 Conference is symptomatic of this outlook, as shown by the following remarks by the municipal authorities:

Lille : "The university has not yet made a big enough effort even though we feel we have not lagged behind in the Nord/Pas-de-Calais."

Dijon : "These institutions ought to make an effort to adapt their teaching to economic needs..."

Metz : "At the present stage of redeployment and diversification in Lorraine, the university should train technical and managerial staff and help, with its research, to develop new products able to compete on the world market..."

Rouen : "Over and above its teaching role, the university can and must act as a stimulus to the regional economy."

Orsay : "The present situation is one more illustration of the criticism often levelled at the university that it does not fit into the world around it. This fact is too obvious to be anything but deliberate policy... the university should come to the municipality – not the reverse."

Angers : "The university needs to draw up an action programme and select priority areas in which the local community might provide financial aid for research"

Créteil : "The university acts towards the municipal authorities like a 'petitioner without a cause' in the feeble hope of material or financial support"

Marseille : "Although increasingly open to its environment, the university is still something of an ivory tower"

Chambéry : "The university's capacity to make proposals for collaboration is more effective than requests from the local authorities

Lyon : "The university is still too often introverted; industrial circles and policy-makers have not so far tried to forge a structural link with higher education

These results and comments may seem unexpected. They are nevertheless confirmed by surveys carried out in other Member countries. It is admittedly difficult to interpret such information when it comes from the United States or Sweden because the term "university initiative" may in fact be a proposal by the "Board of Trustees" or the various community representatives in the university.

What is more, the figure given (52.5 per cent) needs refining. Which, for example is the most dynamic group in the higher educational institution – students, teachers or executive body? In some cases, it is formed by the students. In Denmark, for instance, the opening of experimental libraries at Naestved and Aalborg with the help of the local municipal libraries was due to the students at the Copenhagen School of Librarians and the Aalborg Royal College of Librarians, assisted by a state grant. In other cases, the initiative has come from teachers at the same or other universities. Thus, four teachers belonging to four different universities in Canada and the United States (University of Waterloo, University of Toronto, University of Wisconsin and Michigan State University) took the initiative of launching an activity to produce proposals for restoring the eco-systems of the Great Lakes. The Great Lakes Fishery Commission thereupon commissioned a study and this was delivered in June 1979. Forty-eight people from several universities and from various institutions concerned with environmental problems contributed.

Many more examples could be given of pioneer academics who accept the inherent risks of enterprise and make the effort of convincing a few colleagues and obtaining the support of their universities. There is indeed a risk that the activity will remain marginal if the department or university does not give the proposal enough backing or if the "customers" are not in a position to provide the necessary financial support. This marginalisation of an activity, in which an individual and not an institution is committed, is a classic development which tends to perpetuate the traditional situation in the name of academic independence.

Initiative is also quite closely linked with the administrative framework. In France, for example, only "the University" is a legal entity. The departments and the teaching and research units thus find it very difficult to enter into contracts and sign agreements. The "university autonomy" guaranteed by the 1968 Act is offset by centralising machinery within each university which could well inhibit the flexibility needed in relations with the community. There is no doubt that, when the university takes the initiative in an activity, or gives it official backing, this is a real commitment indicating a genuine intention to work for the benefit of the community.

The number of activities launched on the *initiative of local/regional communities* is, nevertheless, considerable (23.5 per cent).

The term "community initiative" also presents certain problems.

Are the authorities involved local or regional? If these authorities are themselves an emanation of the central power (the regional physical planning agencies in France or the prefects of the corresponding authorities in Portugal or Spain and the different Federal agencies in the United States), is the term "local initiative" still applicable?

If a local or group initiative is involved, it nearly always originates with a leading citizen or a group of eminent people who have themselves been to university and know what may be expected of it. Can this be described as a "community" initiative?

Last but not least, any specific community consists of groups or strata which are, to varying extents, complementary or in conflict, representing the community, administrative area units, firms, associations, trade unions and minority groups. Do not community initiatives carry over the conflicts or ambiguities characterising the community itself into the university?

Conversely, when referring to university initiatives, is there not a tendency to forget that members of a university, whether faculty or students, are also part of the community? When a teacher proposes participation in an educational programme, does he do so only as a researcher or as a pupil's parent? When another puts forward a programme of action concerned with the environment, is it as an expert or as a citizen suffering from the same disamenities – or sometimes the prisoner of the same myths – as his fellow citizens?

In some countries, the *national authorities* are *increasingly* (16 per cent) encouraging community-linked activities. This is true of the United States, France, Portugal and Sweden.

The United States is an interesting example. Under the Higher Education Act, Title I, Community Service and Continuing Education, Congress established a partnership between Federal State and post-secondary educational institutions with the object of providing the community with continuing education facilities and services designed to help the community solve its problems. "Community service program means an educational program activity on service offered by an institution of higher education and designed to assist in the solution of community problems in rural, urban or suburban areas with particular emphasis on urban and suburban problems". This definition is given in the 1975 assessment of the program under the first Title of the Act. In spite of varying interpretations of this Act, the following are some common assumptions which must be considered in assessing the Title I program:

- Post-secondary institutions represent valuable resources which, if properly stimulated, mobilised and applied, could assist people in solving problems;
- Title I should support programs for adults to help them solve community problems rather than for purely personal benefit or self-enrichment;
- Problems, although national in scope, must be solved in a regional or community setting;
- Institutional participation in the program should be based on ability, willingness and commitment to deal with specific problems;
- Educational institutions must share with communities the task of determining problem areas and authorities to which educational assistance should be applied;
- Title I should modify traditional educational missions and result in new or stronger community service/continuing education programs;
- State agencies through their administrative and planning functions should provide sufficient co-ordination to offset problems that might otherwise occur in such a broad-gauged program. Decision about projects to be supported and the extent of institutional participation should be a function of the State's management of the program.

Article 24 of the French Higher Education Act (1968) is more restrictive but points in the same direction when it says that "the universities shall organise lifelong education in the teaching and research units which they set up in institutions attached to them and in the services they create for this purpose. This activity shall be organised in liaison with regional and local communities, public institutions and any other interested bodies".

This encouragement at the national level may stimulate initiative, whether from the university or the community, but it may also be inhibiting through not taking sufficient account of the differences between local and regional situations.

Lastly, apart from legislation, it must be noted that what is sometimes called government initiative is really nothing more than that of a person holding high enough office in the Administration.

We ought also to mention *initiatives at international level,* which are generally combined with one or more proposals from various public or private, national or local institutions, including a number of universities. International organisations play an important part in such initiatives to which they often give financial support.

We put activities launched by a combination of initiatives in a last category. These generally consist of a series of individual actions taken by institutions that are going to be partners in the future activity. Prompted by a request, an approach or a need, one particular person belonging to a given body attempts to win the support of other persons in various other university or community bodies who, in their respective spheres, then take the initiative in the activity concerned. An illustration is the project on "University Continuing Education" in Southern Italy. The initiative came jointly, in 1972, from the Giulio Pastore Foundation and a public agency – the FORMEZ (training and study centre for the Mezzogiorno). After intensive preliminary studies, a research project was developed in 1976/7 in the gravitation centres of the Bari and Salerno universities, forming a new partnership, with a contribution from the EEC Commission and some co-ordination with the Catholic University of Milan and the Charleroi Open University.

In the previous chapter, we described and interpreted the various specific university-community liaison bodies. Some of these undoubtedly facilitate the emergence of initiative.

Such is the case for the "system" set up by the City College of the City University of New York. In 1979 the university published an interesting document entitled "The City College Community Collaboration Procedure Manual", which the Vice-President for Academic Affairs prefaced with these words: "Since 1847, when it first opened its doors to the citizens of New York City as the Free Academy, City College has served the educational needs of the urban community. To-day, as part of its urban mission, City College continues to provide broad opportunity and a quality education to a representative student body drawn from all parts of the City. It also seeks, through research and service, to expand and enhance its collaborative interaction with the community. This manual is designed to facilitate such collaboration".

In other words, regardless of the source of the initiative, a participation and decision-making system has to be set up as is clearly explained in the introduction to the Manual: "the urban university model requires the full and relevant participation of the community in the activities of the City College, and the availability of the institutional resources of the college to the community. Such participation requires co-operation and interaction in timely fashion between community groups and the college, and among various units of the college: schools, committees, programs, pedagogical and administrative departments and centres. A process and a set of procedures is required in order to expedite decision-making, ensure the relevancy of the activity to the goals and objectives of the college, and to integrate appropriate activities across programs, departments, schools and centres... This participation can be initiated by four entities: community representatives, students, faculty and administrators. For each initiating entity there is a procedure that assures clear decision-making, accountability and right of appeal."

This remarkable manual, which lays down procedures for any of the four groups wishing to initiate an activity is the product of long experience of university/community relations whose exact forms had to be defined over the course of time.

The example is interesting since it seems to avoid the contradiction between highly decentralised and flexible structures, which facilitate the emergence of individual and collective initiatives but inhibit decision-making and implementation, and centralised bureaucratic structures which, conversely, inhibit initiative but accelerate decision-making and implementation.

The customary conflict between these two approaches explains why, in the last chapter, we avoided concentrating on one type of mechanism rather than another and preferred to describe them in all their diversity. The City College's original solution seems to show that it is possible, in practice, to associate highly flexible participation strategies with planned development models. It is based on very close integration of the College in its environment, coupled with a very strict conception of university autonomy.

2. FINANCING OF ACTIVITIES

As in all sectors of public life, the financing aspect is important. Apart from the scale of resources available to develop projects for the benefits of the community, however, some fundamental questions again surface connected either with the autonomy or dependence of the university in relation to the community, with the accounts to be rendered to the financing sources or with the insidious process of the conversion of the university into a rapidly expanding "service-station" (as some of the cases analysed in the previous chapter might suggest). Moreover, the question of financing service activities is related to countries' general policies of university development in a period of economic austerity and diminishing resources for higher education.

In the survey we carried out, we endeavoured to ascertain the origin of the finance for these activities by suggesting three main possibilities and one combined source: Firstly, the higher educational institution (sub-question: what percentage of the institutions's budget?), secondly the community, thirdly, public or private grants and, lastly, a combination of these various possibilities (what percentage in each case?). The 119 institutions in 22 Member countries gave 158 replies to this question on financing, broken down as follows into the various categories mentioned:

- 56 replies (about 35.5 per cent): mainly state financing;
- 48 replies (about 30 per cent): higher educational institutions as the main source of finance;
- 43 replies (about 27.5 per cent): local regional community – including firms – as the principal source of finance;
- 11 replies (about 7 per cent): combinations of the above.

It can thus be seen that the funds for the activities are drawn in fairly equal proportions from the higher educational sector, the local community, and the state authorities, the last-named being in the lead. The figures relate only to the chief source of funds, further money coming from the other sources mentioned, in the form, more particularly, of grants in certain countries.

Seven per cent – i.e. very few activities – are financed by a combination of different sources of funds. Here it may be a question of a deliberate policy to involve all the parties concerned in a project up to and including the financing aspect.

An example in this connection is the University of Louisville, Kentucky, United States, which reports the following proportions in financing sources for its "Urban Study Centre": 33 per cent state government, 28 per cent university, 19 per cent local authorities, 13 per cent federal government and 7 per cent private donations and other sources. It can be seen that this breakdown follows the previous pattern, i.e. even in the case of a combination of financing sources, public finance (46 per cent in this case) is the mainspring.

Mention has already been made of Title I of the 1965 Higher Education Act, designed to develop community projects in the United States. To be specific, the government authorised an allocation of 285 million dollars for the period 1966-1973 ; 83 million dollars were distributed during that period to 1 214 colleges and universities (representing nearly half the higher educational institutions in the country) ; 314 projects were supported in 1967, 501 in 1970 and 731 in 1973. Two points are worth noting. Firstly, the State Universities and the Land Grant Colleges, representing only 22 per cent of the total number of institutions participating, receive 46 per cent of the total funds.

Secondly, the proportion represented by the Community Colleges grew very rapidly from 12 per cent (38 institutions) in 1967 to 32 per cent (236 institutions) in 1973.

The various States were required to share in the financing of these projects. In actual fact, of the 46 million dollars which supplemented the 83 million from the federal government, roughly 82 per cent were provided by the institutions, 12 per cent by the States and local governments, and the remainder by private donation. "Although the matching funds are provided on a State-wide basis, the pattern throughout the program has been to generate matching funds from institutions. This constitutes a major commitment by institutions to the community problem-solving efforts of Title I".

This financing policy, the policy of incentive at the central level, seems to have given satisfactory results to judge by the conclusion reached by the National Advisory Council on Extension and Continuing Education on the first question asked in the evaluation exercise: "Has Title I resulted in a signicant number of colleges and universities directing more of their efforts towards solving community problems?".

Conclusion: "The Title I Program has demonstrated its ability to induce institutions to contribute resources to assisting people and communities to solve problems. In addition to providing those institutions which had capacities in extension and continuing education to pursue new directions, it has also introduced other colleges and universities to community outreach and added to the total number of institutions providing assistance to communities.

This example from the United States clearly shows the positive incentive role which the central authority can and should play, provided that the institutions are left some room for manœuvre. The interesting reports supplied by the School of Education of Malmö University in Sweden following a Seminar (in which other university institutions from Lund, and community representatives, participated) points out that "basic training is almost entirely financed by State grants... In-service training within the School of Education is also purely the concern of the State authorities". The authors' comments are as follows: "the extent and nature of co-operation between the School and other bodies with regard to basic and further training has up to now been strongly influenced by policy decisions of the central authorities regarding curricula. Admittedly, it has not been obligatory to follow these instructions in every detail, but in practice they have had a dominant influence. As a result the majority of contacts that have been established between the school of education and other organisations have been primarily directed to the needs of the school and not the other way round. In the higher education reform that would come into effect as from 1 July 1977, mutual co-operation can more readily be instigated at the local level, as a result of which these contracts will, hopefully, develop both quantitatively and qualitatively".

If, then, this freedom of action is preserved, in spite of the main financial contributions coming from the central authorities, it may be wondered whether, conversely, a small or non-existent financial participation by the local/regional communities could not cause them to dissociate themselves on any activities in which they might be involved. However this may be, both the university and the local/regional communities agree upon the need for a financial contribution from those communities to any project intended to solve some of their problems and difficulties. The very full investigation carried out by California University at Irvine in conjunction with the CERI in 1977, both within the University (by internal questionnaire) and in its surrounding community (external questionnaire) reveals a measure of agreement between the two parties on this point which by no means extends to all the subjects of the survey.

The question was as follows: "does the community have a responsibility to assist in financing those UCI programs and facilities that are designed to serve the community's needs?". The pattern of the replies was as follows:

External questionnaire (local community)		Internal questionnaire (university)
18.7 %	Agree strongly	32 %
43.1 %	Agree to some extent	37 %
8.5 %	Undecided	11 %
10.8 %	Disagree to some extent	9.7 %
13.6 %	Disagree strongly	5.1 %
5.1 %	No opinion	4.2 %

(179 people in the community and 235 in the university answered the questionnaire which was the same in both cases). While the total percentage of those who were on the

whole in agreement is 61.8 per cent in the community and 69 per cent in the University, it is natural to find that 32 per cent in the University, compared with 18.7 per cent in the community, were strongly in favour of the community providing finance. There are few surprises in these figures.

The complex of groups making up a community, and the various levels of service, make this question of financing somewhat complicated once the attempt is made to go beyond the above general considerations. A relevant example is the problem of continuing training, where often, rather than there being a problem of financing, the activity may be lucrative for the university concerned in certain countries. It is said, for example, that in France, in view of the universities' financial difficulties, the latter are willy-nilly obliged to go in for "life-saving operations" by organising continuous training. The University of Haute Alsace at Mulhouse, for example, which contains 1 934 students has research contracts – half of them with semi-public agencies, the other half with business firms – worth 3½ million francs. The total budget is 11½ million francs of which the lion's share – 6½ million – comes from continuous training. The Louis Pasteur University at Strasbourg, also in France, with 13 000 students, half of them studying medicine, has a total budget of 94 million francs. Medical subsidies cover only 27 million and the other 67 million are produced by large-scale business in analytical laboratories.

When continuing training or applied research activities are not carried out to earn profits for the departments concerned or other departments in the university, they are generally financed on a contractual basis between the partners. The services supplied by the Swedish universities to the members of the Swedish Confederation of Trade Unions (LO) are an example: the universities bear the teaching costs while the unions make up participants' loss of earnings and pay their travel and accommodation expenses.

CONCLUSION

Regarding initiative

The above classification of where the initiative originates (university, local/regional community including trade unions and firms, central authorities, foundations, international bodies or a combination of any of these) must be treated with caution for the following reasons:

- The initiator of an activity may be very difficult to identify. G. Denielou tells how a student at his university doing in-service training in a firm (and therefore involved in a process of "alternating" education) was faced with problems calling for applied research. The firm then turned to the university for an analysis of these problems. These "services" were negotiated by the student, who had been instrumental in revealing the need for the research. He was also the researcher – through the doctorate thesis he was writing while working in the firm. Should this situation be regarded as spin-off from a university alternating education project, as an "order" from a firm, arising from a personal relationship, or as the pooling of resources?
- Owing to the reduction of their grants in many Member countries, the universities have to find other resources in order to survive and therefore to enter the training and research markets and obey their laws. Can this be called a university approach to the community, an indirect incentive from the public authorities or pressure by the business sector?

- If the initiative is regarded as a response to pressure, the relative strength of the various pressures has to be determined to find out which sector exerts most influence. The relations between the post-secondary sector and the trade unions in Sweden provides an example of the way the key factors interlock. Did the "pressure" come from the 1977 higher education reform or was it brought to bear by the Swedish Confederation of Trade Unions (LO) at central level or by a single trade union at regional level? The answer to this question is in fact of interest only if we are trying to clarify the attitude of the university and the community groups towards new forms of exchanges and co-operation.

Regarding financing

The financing of activities benefiting the community needs to be analysed in far greater detail. Indeed, this type of financing cannot be dissociated from the universities' general financing system and, as already mentioned, is therefore connected with the whole problem of university autonomy, the nature of university functions (teaching, research and service) and the interaction between these functions.

The above comments will appear to confirm the separation mentioned in Chapter 2 between the traditional high-status teaching and research activities and the less exalted service activities of continuing education and applied research. Very approximately there would thus appear to be a special type of financing, to which the recent principle of "accountability" would not apply, for the traditional, high-status activities and another kind of financing for service activities requiring immediate accountability to financial backers. Martin Trow made a similar distinction in 1975 between the university's "autonomous functions" and its "popular functions". But since the state universities are financed out of the national budget and taxpayers are demanding more control over the spending they pay for with the object of ensuring their needs are better catered for out of these public funds, it may well be asked how the distinction between these autonomous functions and popular functions can be maintained and whether it should in fact be maintained.

The study of the financing of the university's various activities in the current period of recession is the subject of recent research, not least in the United States where the problem is acute for both the private and state universities alike, both anxious to find public and private funds as pointed out by Martin Kramer in his recent book "The Venture Capital of Higher Education" [32].

This transition from strict control of the utilisation of funds granted for specific action to overall inspection of all university activities explains and justifies the hesitation of certain "traditional" universities to engage in service activities. Indeed, if continuing training activities were dictated by employers' requirements, all basic training policy might ultimately be geared to the exigencies of the employment market alone. This is hardly acceptable to the university.

Martin Kramer makes a distinction which seems fundamental between "accountability to the future" and "accountability to the present". A great many of the activities under the "services" heading are attempted responses to cyclical situations. It is therefore possible and necessary to determine their "accountability". The same "accountability" criteria can hardly be applied to continuing education and research activities.

The existence of two types of financing, linked with two types of "accountability", – regardless of whether the funds come from public or private sources – therefore entails the risk of a form of control based on criteria of immediate effectiveness and acceptability to the social system being extended to all university activity. This extension could be defined as "accountability to the future" being completely ousted by "accountability to the present" or, put another way, would mean that "popular functions" would once and for all, take precedence over "autonomous functions".

Since financing is the expression and means of prior control by society, it is a way of measuring to what extent the growth of activities in the interests of the community is an opportunity or a danger for higher education.

Part Three

STRUCTURAL CHANGES
IN THE UNIVERSITY
BECAUSE OF ITS CHANGING FUNCTIONS

Chapter 1

INSTITUTIONAL STRUCTURES,
CONTENT AND TEACHING METHODS

It is not the purpose of this chapter to examine the interactions between higher education and the community but to trace the effects of the increase in these interactions on higher education. We shall therefore be dealing with only one of the terms of the confrontation, the one which is no doubt the more homogeneous and which lends itself better to comparative analysis in spite of the differences in different countries' higher education systems.

We shall therefore attempt a systematic inventory of the observable effects on higher education of its intensifying relations with its environment. This inventory will enable us to define the fabric of institutional, education and scientific practices in which the trend for links with the community to grow is developing.

The repercussions we have been able to observe and study are of two kinds. The first affects the *structures* and *institutional operation* of the universities and can be seen either in the creation of new structures or in changes to the *modus operandi* of existing institutions.

The second relates mainly to *teaching* in its wide sense and affects the organisation of studies and curricula, teaching methods and syllabuses.

1. INSTITUTIONAL EFFECTS

Unification or diversification of the higher education system?

A large variety of higher education institutions is to be observed in OECD countries and that variety increased during the sixties with the considerable increase in the number of university students. It would not appear that thinking about co-ordination with the community was the reason for specific research into the character and organisation of these institutions except in the earlier cases of the Land Grant Universities and, more recently, the Community Colleges in the United States or the Regional Colleges in Scandinavia. It is true that, in most countries, attention has been given to local and regional considerations in plotting the "university map". Vocational training institutions, for example, have been set up to meet the needs of the local economy and the presence of representatives of the local communities on the governing boards of higher education institutions has been encouraged and sometimes made mandatory although the organisational and administrative consequences have not all been taken to their logical conclusion.

In the United Kingdom, the philosophy governing the creation of the polytechnics was a response to the requirements and demands of the community but our survey showed that there were wide variations from one polytechnic to another and that some universities were equally concerned about their social and economic environment.

At all events we consider that the increase in partnerships with the community has two consequences that are only apparently in conflict with one another.

The first consequence seems to be an accentuation in the differences between institutions, and more particularly between universities and other higher education institutions, but also between large and small institutions of similar status. Whilst universities work at a more theoretical and fundamental level, colleges, polytechnics, university institutes of technology, etc. are mainly concerned with know-how and technological development. The larger institutions monopolise the activities of national or international importance whereas the smaller institutions, simply because of their location, devote themselves more to the problems of their immediate environment. This is particularly noticeable in the case of research and accentuates the division between two kinds of research, the one being pure, superior, fundamental, universal and suffering no constraints, which is the preserve of the universities and certain specialised institutions, and the other being "impure", secondary, applied and local – the province of other post-secondary institutions. This distinction is sometimes intended by the legislature itself. In 1967, the Secretary of State for Education and Science in the United Kingdom described his Government's concept of research in polytechnics in these terms: "the main responsibility of the polytechnics will be as teaching institutions, but it will be necessary to make the provision for research which is essential to the proper fulfilment of their teaching functions and the maintenance and development of close links with industry, particularly local industry, so as to promote the rapid application of results to its problems" [33].

The second consequence is the quest for better co-ordination between different institutions since it very seldom seems to lead to unified structures. This is particularly true when the development of links with the community tends to favour regional and local interests. Most of the institutions which took part in the CERI survey agree that the development of coherent regular activity with the community may force the various partners to co-operate with each other, work as a team in accordance with individual locations and skills, share out tasks, etc.

Some studies, particularly in Canada and Australia, stress the fact that links with the community create conditions for co-operation between universities, colleges and schools aimed at avoiding pointless competition and the duplication of teaching, resources and expenditure. In the United States, the emergence of planning machinery is reported which sometimes teams public and private institutions in joint harness. The University of Texas, for example, has a fully-fledged research organisation for improving these links, studying the problems involved and proposing changes on the university side to help it to provide more appropriate facilities.

In France, institutions of different kinds and with different functions and origins are found to be co-ordinating their activities, thanks mainly to the "regional planning boards (missions régionales d'aménagement) whose job it is to plan regional development in the main programme regions (régions de programme), of which there are 17 covering 95 Départements. Some of these institutions are of private and others of government origin and they have come to co-ordinate their efforts and research work. This kind of co-ordination at regional level, which involves no movement towards unification, is featured in a study by the University of Aix-Marseille II [34].

In other words, while in most OECD countries institutional diversity has more often been simply the result of competition and successive policy measures – the less coherent as, although it is easy to create new institutions, it is much rarer for insitutions to disappear entirely even when they have not fulfilled their purpose – the development of policies centred on the community prescribes specific functions and calls for co-ordination, which in turn, helps to clarify situations.

In the United States a number of original forms of inter-institutional co-operation are found, e.g. "consortia" for specific programmes. Some of these consortia are discussed at length in Part Two, Chapter 2. The consortium arrangement broadens the approach to problems concerning one or more "local communities" and the scope for solving them. Such co-operation between different institutions also enables more financial and human resources to be tapped. Co-operation between several institutions makes them better able to tackle the problems raised by the community and to concentrate more resources on them.

The internal development of institutions is much more confused...
as the examples of university-community interaction have already shown.

An institution – especially a university – is seldom wholly committed to developing relations with its environment.

There are three possible situations:

– *The first,* an old pattern, is the growth of unofficial contacts. Individuals and groups inside and outside higher education institutes build up their contacts, solicit research contracts, offer training facilities and widen the range of courses. Generally the procedure for negotiating arrangements for vocational training, continuous training, education for the general population and applied research is left to the initiative of individuals, a group of teachers or a department, and the institution only intervenes when they are put into operation. This is how the Universities of Ryokoku and Kyoto in Japan, for example, organise their activities. The interest teachers take in how the community functions depends on their abilities and on how keen their interests.

– *Secondly,* as we have seen, the university will set up special structures for its dealings with the community. These arrangements may confer differing degrees of independence and involve the rest of the institution to varying extents. Almost all United States institutions, for example, have – in addition to their "extension services" – special arrangements for improving their relations with the outside world, and in all the universities there is a Vice-President in charge of these relations. Such structures develop numerous types of action but these generally remain external to the parent institution; they have no effect on the traditional components of the system which, at both educational and research levels, remain the most important and prestigious parts of the university. The staff do not perceive their community activities as part of their university career. Structures of this kind tend gradually to become more specialised and acquire their own financial resources and staffs. The departments, offices and committees responsible for relations with the community gradually begin to duplicate the institutional structures without really interacting with them. In other words, in spite of their number and diversity, relations with the community may be highly superficial and one of the effects of instituting these special arrangements may be to establish a sort of buffer area protecting the static and enduring character of the rest of the university and preventing "service" functions from interfering with its traditional teaching and research functions.

This is not always true and, in a *third case*, the university authorities will decide that the whole university must participate in relations with the community. These relations then spill over onto all university activities thus affecting its curricula, methods and structures.

119

This may not necessarily be a voluntary choice but a result of a change in the student population. The number of part-time students and adult students (who therefore support themselves and are in permanent jobs) is increasing everywhere and this change in the university population is affecting its policy, a phenomenon which, of itself, accelerates the process. The number of traditional students seems likely to decline in the eighties and the university will then be tempted to engage in different or hitherto neglected activities, such as serving different publics, in particular older students, minorities, etc. This new orientation will have repercussions on a university's internal structures because the traditional training and research system itself will be confronted with a number of specific demands from the community whereas such demands used to be referred to separate organisations, independent of normal educational and research facilities.

The choice of one or other of the three patterns we have listed (unofficial contacts, more or less independent specialised facilities, whole university or institution) is not just a matter of form. Not only does it condition the depth and extent of the implications of these relations for teaching (which we shall consider later) but it also determines how the community can approach a higher education institution and play its part in facilities established by the latter to communicate with it.

Siting of universities and their relations with the community: concerted town or region/university development

Some of the implications of the fast-developing links between the universities and their environment may be regarded as institutional and concern location.

It was seen in Part One, Chapter 1 that the isolated campus or the multi-location university with no co-ordination at the level of objectives, responsibilities and management was a barrier to the university's integration in and commitment to the community.

Various new models hinging on the key concept of *concerted town/region university development* have thus been brought in by Member countries. The common feature, though to varying degrees, is the policy of integrating the university's social and educational facilities with those of the community. The integration of facilities in these models has a twofold objective: to avoid the waste of resources caused by duplicating expensive facilities particularly in the present period of economic crisis and to make encounters and exchanges possible between different social classes and age groups and between students and academics, or in other words to organise permeability between the university and its environment.

The following examples illustrate the various possible combinations of old or new universities with old or new towns.

- *New university – old town.* Even though the period of intensive university building is now over in most OECD countries, there are some recent cases not based on the campus model. One is the University of Technology, Compiègne (France) set up in 1972. The University's guidebook, entitled "une université intégrée à une ville moyenne", describes the integration of the university community with the town as one of the main guiding principles governing the siting of the university. Its restaurants, cultural centres, libraries, living accommodation, offices and sports facilities are twinned with those of the town. "The perennial source of this outgoing approach is the idea of participating in every sphere of civic life whilst remaining unobstrusive and ensuring gradual integration while encouraging initiative from every person."
- *New university – new town.* Roskilde in Denmark, Hiroshima in Japan and Louvain-la-Neuve in Belgium illustrate this policy of town/university integration in varying situations and reflect its failures, ambiguities and realities.

Failure in the case of Roskilde because the integrated new town/university centre project was finally jettisoned, a serious setback, as Mr. Carton notes [35], to the opening up of the university to the community in a new type of relationship.

The transfer of Hiroshima University in Japan to the new town of Higashi Hiroshima illustrates a different approach to integration from the earlier examples. The student revolt in 1969 on the Hiroshima campus had awakened awareness of the need for reform in the educational and research structures. The re-siting of the university seemed, at that time, to be an essential feature of this reform. It was therefore decided in 1973 to move the university to the new town of Higashi Hiroshima: "New town for education and research" [36], in other words a system in which the university would be the main part and a town would be integrated – taking things to extremes – in the university. The "New academic town of Tsukuba" is based on the same model. In spite of the ambiguities, the two above examples are interesting cases of integrated town/university development.

Louvain-la-Neuve in Belgium – the last example under this heading – is clearly a success in many respects although the forecasts about the growth development of the town did not come true. M. Woitrin [37] reports that the whole town was so planned that it could adapt flexibly to the new functions of the university, i.e. new responsibilities, re-training and lifelong education, contacts with wider sections of the public, a university for retired people, a regionally-minded approach, etc.

– *Old university – old town.* This last model of concerted development is particularly interesting for, as will be seen, it shows that urban and university structures with, in some cases, several centuries of history behind them can perfectly well start to move and change when there is an active desire for integration on both sides. This can lead to the pooling of existing resources and more particularly of existing living accommodation. There are many examples, e.g. Leiden in the Netherlands, Bologna in Italy, Louvain in Belgium and also in Great Britain, where old houses have been renovated and given to those students not finding accommodation with families or else small student homes have been built in the town. But the example of the University of Pavia, Italy, shows how an old university (founded in 1361) already a part of the urban and regional structure of the town of Pavia, can be transformed so as to meet social, economic, cultural and regional objectives. This change is being brought about on the basis of a General University Development and Re-structuring Plan (De Carlo Plan), proposed in 1974 and now being implemented. It is underpinned by an in-depth study of the role of the university in the town and in the region. In this successful multipolar and dispersed system, objectives, responsibilities and management of the various parts are closely co-ordinated and the facilities either integrated with those of the community or made available to it.

The above examples show that the integration of the university in its social context can take different forms. In each solution the advantages also imply drawbacks: the multi-location, dispersed university that has split up in order to blend into the social environment may increase the fragmentation of its disciplines by geographical dispersal. Each solution will depend on the historical, economic and structural characteristics of the country concerned. There is, however, one characteristic common to all: the desire on the part of the university and the community to put an end to isolation and segregation by concerted regional and urban development and a more logical use of university and community resources.

As a last comment, it must be stressed that the institutional implications of university location only arise if it performs all three functions: teaching, research and service. The physical separation of the university from its environment has little significance in the case of a fundamental research centre particularly in the exact sciences. But is university the right term in this case? Is it not simply a "specialised research centre"? Again comparison could be made with the "open university", where it makes no difference whether the university is located in a town or a suburb since the aim is "long-distance" teaching. Here the same question arises: is this still a "university" or merely a "long-distance teaching unit"?

2. CURRICULA AND TEACHING METHODS

The variety that is theoretically possible in teaching methods and in the ways they might be changed is even greater than in the case of institutional machinery and therefore only a very highly condensed description can be given of them. It is, in any case, difficult to identify changes and innovations in teaching connected with closer relations with the community. The point is that one and the same reform project is aimed simultaneously at changes in teaching methods and at the strengthening of these relations, without it being possible to establish any cause-and-effect relationship between the two. It is also important to bear cultural factors in mind since university traditions vary widely from country to country. Some countries regard change in teaching methods as a revolution. Ideas like working in small groups, teaching centred on projects and sandwich courses are novelties which began to appear in France, for example, in 1965 but in Portugal only in 1974. In other countries, these methods are almost normal, so that it is difficult to say how far their introduction is connected with the development of relations with the community. However we have been able to identify three main types of "change", a term that seems to be preferable to "innovation" because, in most cases, there is no evaluation enabling us to state that the change is for the better.

Changes in the organisation of curricula

Two major changes should be noted with reference to the general scheme of university/community relations.
- *The growth of so-called alternating education.* In general, alternating education has been regarded as a means of facilitating relations between the university and the community (cf. Part One, Chapter 4). It is believed to facilitate dialogue and exchanges on a more objective and practical basis.
  In fact, the system comes up against many difficulties:
  - its unsuitability for some of training (literary, legal and scientific subjects); institutional obstacles and the "unreality" of the time spent by students in the community or in firms. With no real position, students form false ideas about the part they really play in the host organisation;
  - theoretical obstacles: the facts and experiments are not meaningful in themselves. In order to interpret, combine and rank them, the student needs conceptual tools and methodological instruments. Theory is seldom a matter of merely formalising experience, and if the contacts with practical life are too fleeting and ill-prepared, the student may be deluded regarding his knowledge and made allergic to a critical attitude;

- if alternating education is not to be just a teaching "kit", it has to be placed in the wider context of liaison between university and community because it calls for thorough preparation by the student and the host community whether the latter is a firm or other kind of organisation.
- *A new distribution of theoretical and practical forms of training and the existence of direct contact with practical life from the moment training starts.* This is apparent in systems of de facto alternating education when adult students with working experience enter a university.

Going further, however, a change in relations with the community would imply that the environment should not be regarded as a field of application for previously acquired knowledge but as a place for really learning, diagnosing real problems and exchanging experience. In the experiments we have been able to study, some of the training is indeed given outside the training institution. Here again, what is required is not simply to try out what one has learnt, but to acquire the varying knowledge and experience that is needed both for vocational training and for personal fulfilment and the development of a critical sense.

Changes in the content of higher education

Changes in content seem, to us, to have three main effects.

- *Firstly, more inter- or multidisciplinary projects.* Interdiciplinarity is both the foundation and the stumbling block of training based on the development of relations with the community. Every real problem is, by definition, multi-referential, involving – at one and the same time – at one and the same time – several actors, institutions and fields of activity, these being varyingly structured and at various levels – economic, social and cultural.

The experiments that we have been able to study are numerous, ranging from profound institutional changes to informal co-operation between disciplines or, even more simply, between persons. They all assume a strict pursuit of disciplines as well as a systematic interrogation of their boundaries and a mutual enlightenment of knowledge and policies which breaks down the traditional boundaries by demanding new standards of knowledge. Thus, each time, we encounter threee types of question:

- about the disciplines themselves;
- about the relationship between theory and practice; and about the relationship between social practice and science for its own sake.

The following chapter highlights the importance of interdisciplinarity as both an educational approach and a condition for change in the university's functions and social status.

- *Secondly, the emergence of a new balance between the fundamental disciplines and the increased share of the humanities and social sciences.* The last point leads into this second observation. While labour market logic is tending to reduce the flow of students towards the social sciences, their orientation towards the practical problems of the community brings out the continuing importance of political, economic, sociological and psychological factors. The emergence of these disciplines is directly connected with an awareness of the social function (in the wider sense of the term, which includes development, culture, the economy, etc.) of higher education. At the same time the way in which these disciplines are contemplated inevitably leads to misunderstanding if not conflict. After all, the community is asking to be provided with real "social technologies" the necessary results of which would be to set up normative procedures. The process by which higher education takes these factors into account must necessarily be one of interrogation and criticism. In other words the development of university/community relations must bring about (a) changes in the balance between disciplines and in their most conventional combination and (b) a latent conflict regarding the use that may be made of them in the context of the university.

- *Thirdly, the link between content and a certain kind of "intervention" in the field.* In addition, the procedures of interdisciplinarity are directly connected with what was discussed under the heading "the response of higher education" at the February 1980 Conference. Whereas a "service" function in the strict sense implies the adoption of interdisciplinary practices, in other words a more or less closely knit assemblage of pieces of knowledge and skill (of which the traditonal training of engineers and even physicians is quite a good example), taking part in a study of the problems and demands of the community calls for a combination of knowledge and methods which is far more complex and based on practice, the term applied to it by the CERI in past studies being "transdisciplinary".

Changes in methods and the teaching "relationship"

Project-based teaching, combined research/learning, working in small groups, team learning, extra-mural studies, indeed a full range of conventional and unconventional teaching practices seem to be associated with the problem of co-operation with the community. Generally speaking, the ones employed seem to be those lumped together under the heading of "active teaching methods." Some universities insist that when such methods have practical targets, they should be applied not only to the traditional type of student from a secondary school but also to adults whose grasp of the needs of the community and ability to co-operate with the community enlarge the scope for such teaching and improve co-operation. Many, on the hand, elaborate on the difficulties of introducing such innovations because of the opposition of university institutions and that of a number of teachers – especially the senior ones – and also some opposition from members of the community, either because their expectations or demands are too great to be met by the efforts of students, or because the community refuses to be a guinea-pig for studies and experiments by young adults or students from the university.

The development of this type of learning may have profound consequences. From the student's point of view, there is a radical change in traditional practice, particularly in the case of work "in the field". Faced with practical problems rooted in social reality, and in actual touch with possible beneficiaries, students have to arrive at solutions which are acceptable to all – and practicable – and not just to pass an examination. At the same time they must not confuse the rules of scientific objectivity with unanimous or majority voting procedures in a group or scientific approach with empirical approximation.

In other words, these practices seem legitimate to us only to the extent that they require and facilitate a return to theory and therefore only when they are conducive to a training dialectic which itself may lead to further study of how to establish continuity between initial training and lifelong training.

Meanwhile, the frequency of these new teaching practices, together with the development of co-operation with the local environment shows the danger of replacing scientific by pedagogic positivism and, on the pretext of effectiveness and practical value, of exposing students to the confusion of instant information by detaching them from the ascetic problems of research. Here again the key question is at what level the university should act, as a "service station" or as a centre of analysis and objective criticism (cf. Part One, Chapter 2). Both cases involve relations with the environment and the application to society of a scientific method but the two approaches are profoundly different.

However, all these changes in teaching methods make it possible to state that the development of relations with the community has encouraged higher education institutions to diversify their teaching and research and thereby extend their range of methods and teaching techniques. Some institutions, for example, have gradually, thanks to the development of these relations, become laboratories for experimenting with the alternation system, the use of team learning methods, models, simulators, etc.

CONCLUSION

Firstly the development of relations between the higher education system – or more precisely in this context the post-secondary education system – and its surrounding community raises two questions of an institutional nature:

– Is the development and growth of relations with the community contributing to an increasing number of more or less parallel higher education institutions that are either in competition or developing specific scientific approaches in each case, or, on the contrary, is it encouraging trends towards the unification or co-ordination of these various institutions?

– Do certain of the existing structures, whose variety has already been referred to, seem more suited than others to improving relations with the community; more particularly, is is possible to confirm or question the time-honoured assumption that institutions offering short courses or technical courses are stucturally better fitted and better oriented to work aimed at the community, in contrast with the universities, generally reputed to be more independent, biased towards the growth of knowledge and having a national if not universal vocation as the name itself reminds us?

Analysis of the various documents and contributions at the February 1980 Conference shows a fairly clear trend: the universities and the other higher education or post-secondary institutions should have specific responsibilities and there should be co-ordination between the various establishments.

Secondly, are there, in the new relations between the university and the community, changes in the very structures of teaching and research and in the teaching system? There is no one answer to this questions; once again a tendency can be observed, that of the creation of new training and research routes, diversity in teaching methods used and enlargement of the range of methodology and teaching in higher education institutions.

These two trends confirm certain proposals which CERI had made in earlier studies for models of "post-secondary structures with regional objectives" which will be referred to in the following chapter under the more specific heading of interdisciplinarity.

Chapter 2

"COMMUNITIES HAVE PROBLEMS, UNIVERSITIES HAVE DEPARTMENTS"

This heading neatly expresses the difficulty a university generally has in responding to an increasing number of requests from the community. The structures of higher education and more particularly the universities are still, for the most part, based on the growth of knowledge and mono-disciplinary practice. When the community brings up complex, and therefore dimensional, situations and asks for multiple action (because a real problem is never exclusively technical, social or scientific), all the university can offer is a collection of analytical structures. Already in 1965, M. Weinberg in *Science* [38] wrote "the mission of society is to solve its variety of problems, virtually none of which could be resolved by the application of a single discipline. The universities on the other hand, rather than being "mission-oriented" are "discipline-oriented". In addition to this the rapid increase in knowledge is tending to lead to an ever-increasing degree of fragmentation and specialisation which in turn is leading to ever-increasing difficulties in communication, which could in time mean that the universities could virtually lose contact with the society which supports them".

So interdisciplinarity is not just a new approach to education and research but the key to the change in the missions and social status of the university. For this reason, interdisciplinarity emerged as a major subject at the OECD Conference in February 1980 and is again the subject of various international meetings and conferences (e.g. the UNESCO Bucharest Colloquium of November 1981 on Interdisciplinarity). Again, because CERI had already carried out an in-depth theoretical exercise in 1969-70 backed up by various concrete studies and surveys on the importance of interdisciplinary education and research.

At that time we proposed some terminological and conceptual clarifications we feel it useful to recall in this chapter.

Discipline: A specific body of teachable knowledge with its own background of education, training procedures, methods and content areas.

Multidisciplinary: Juxtaposition of various disciplines, sometimes with no apparent connection between them. e.g.: music + mathematics + history.

Pluridisciplinary: Juxtaposition of disciplines assumed to be more or less related. e.g.: mathematics + physics, or French + Latin + Greek: "classical humanities" in France.

Interdisciplinary: An adjective describing the *interaction* of two or more different disciplines. This interaction may range from simple communication of ideas to the mutual integration of organising *concepts, methodology, procedures, epistemology, terminology, data,* and organisation of research and education in a fairly large field. An interdisciplinary group consists of persons trained in different fields of knowledge (disciplines) with different concepts, methods, and data and terms organised into a common effort on a common problem with continuous intercommunication among the participants from the different disciplines.

Transdisciplinary: Establishing a common system of axioms for a set of disciplines (e.g. anthropology considered as "the science of man and his accomplishments", according to Linton's definition).

Contributions from various scientists (J. Piaget, the mathematician A. Lichwerowitz and Jantsch) at the OECD Seminar in 1970 made it possible to define the above concepts after in-depth epistemological analysis [39].

This chapter begins by considering the changes that have come about in the demand for interdisciplinarity. Then, using concrete examples, we look at changes in the interdisciplinary content of curricula. Finally, a model for a post-secondary structure that would enable the community's pluridisciplinary requirements and expectations to be met is considered.

1. CHANGES IN THE DEMAND FOR INTERDISCIPLINARITY

In our earlier work, we associated interdisciplinarity with five different types of demand – which could, even so, culminate in similar types of functioning:

The first was linked with the *development of science* though it could take almost contradictory forms.

The first stage is increasing specialisation leading to increasingly restricted fields practically all of which, however, correspond to the meeting point of two disciplines. This intersection helps to demarcate the object but at the same time imposes a multiple approach. Depending on the case, or rather depending on how far the work has advanced, the term used may be interdisciplinarity or new discipline. This tendency for interdisciplinarity to serve, in reality, as the foundation for a new discipline has been observed by many scientists and, in many cases, has even been considered as part of the very purpose and nature of interdisciplinarity. At times, however, they seemed to think that this new discipline should continue to require experts trained in other fields. At other times they really treated interdisciplinarity merely as the symbol of a state of crisis and the means of splitting up an over-rigid discipline at a given moment or setting off into new fields of knowledge. What might be regarded as a variant on this case was the meeting of a given discipline with a particular application stemming from technological progress (e.g. teaching and research in space medicine in the United States, fruit of the development of the biological sciences and of the need to respond to the special problems posed by space flights).

In a reverse trend, this diversification of scientific thought was accompanied by attempts to define a number of common elements. Its first manifestation was an endeavour to maximise science but then came the emergence, on a much more widespread scale, of a number of concepts common to many if not all disciplines such as structure, model, system, etc. In this case, interdisciplinarity was changing into transdisciplinarity.

Without any connection with the development of science, except possibly as a reaction to that development, we emphasized the importance of *"student demand"*. At times this took the form of real pressure but at others it was simply felt by teachers who strove to satisfy it. Most of the time, it was a protest against the fragmentation and artificial subdivision of a reality which it was felt had to be all-embracing and multi-dimensional. In some European countries the protest was intensified by including, at the same time, a reaction to the features of a secondary education that was particularly hidebound, the result of a compartmentation of disciplines that for some times was even stricter than in the traditional university.

In this context, interdisciplinarity was a symbol of "anti-science", a return to a prior experience that was certainly worth analysing provided its basic unity was not overlooked. Discovering that even scientific propositions had political, economic and sociological repercussions thus led to a form of interdisciplinarity. What was involved, clearly, was not the integration but the complementarity of disciplines and, above all, the setting of the objects that each discipline claims to study in real situations. A similar desire to that among students could be observed among the teachers and scientists, a deeply-felt need within their work to meet "those on the outside" even though they could not see the immediate benefit this could be to science. The wish was particularly strong among young teachers. scientists, etc. and was one of the reasons for the friction, on this problem of interdisciplinarity, between professors ensconced in the practice of one homogeneous discipline and their assistants who were far more concerned to be in touch with other disciplines even though this might temporarily slow down their own work.

A third possible origin was the compulsion to put interdisciplinarity into practice in dealing with *problems of university operation or even administration.* The increasingly elaborate equipment in research centres, the need for universities to manage their own budgets and, in some countries, to enter into contracts with a number of organisations meant that those responsible for different departments had to meet and made it essential for university budgets to be managed as economically as possible. In many cases it was the advent of a computer or a contract with the government or with a research agency that forced one university team to make contact with another and to work in joint harness. These problems of management and sharing facilities were particularly interesting because, in this case, interdisciplinarity was directly related to the problem of reorganising and restructuring the university institution. The interdisciplinarity that began in this way generally went on to forget its purely administrative origins and progressed towards problems of a more scientific nature or concerned with the general training of students and scientists.

A very clear distinction has to be made between the above cases and the interdisciplinarity that stemmed from *vocational training requirements* although this was often expressed in terms of demand from students. The term specialist generally does not mean the same thing inside and outside the university. Inside, a specialist works in one discipline or on a tiny aspect of that discipline. In working life, a specialist is almost always someone capable of a combination of approaches to the same reality; there is no such thing as a specialist psychologist but there are industrial psychologists, school psychologists, psychotherapists, etc., in other words on top of a knowledge of psychology there has to be that of business management, education or medicine.

In some cases the attention paid to vocational training or the concern about the practical conditions in which a profession was carried on were caused by the existence of a specific contract between the university, the department, or the team concerned with interdisciplinarity and a specific demand coming either from an outside entity or a specific sector of the environment. In a certain sense, this went beyond vocational training as such into the fifth type of origin, that of an original social demand.

By *original social demand* was meant a number of situations where society as a whole or the local community, the town, region or county, put up to the university new subjects for study which, by definition, could not be contained within any existing disciplinary frame, an example being environmental research.

The increasing extra-university demand for interdisciplinarity

Out of the five types of demand set out above, three were a matter of intra-university development and the two last were one of development in the community.

The requirement that the university should perform its full social mission by multiplying its exchanges with the community means that more weight now has to be given to the development of *interdisciplinarity exogenous to the university,* in other words the interdisciplinarity whose origins are in the continuous momentum provided by the real problems of the community.

A community "problem" prompts the interdisciplinary approach because it acts as a focus unifying the various disciplines concerned. Employment, energy, environment, urban planning, health, transport, etc, these are all problems proposed by communities that open the door to the combination of various disciplines, in particular the natural and human sciences.

Thus it can be seen that this exogenous interdisciplinarity supplements, enriches and interrogates *endogenous university interdisciplinarity,*in other words, the interdisciplinarity based on the production of new knowledge with the aim, more or less explicit, of realising the "unity of science".

Exogenous interdisciplinarity forever questions the disciplines on the validity of the demarcations it applies to real life. If health is the starting point for interrogating the biological sciences then no boundaries can be accepted between physiology and ethology or between biology and psychology. If the starting point is the education problem, this assumes there is an interaction between sociological and psychological aspects, and between the functions of an institution and teaching practice. Similarly, practice in industry cannot simply be seen as applied physics or applied economics.

Each time, therefore, reality has to be approached from different angles and a vital role has to be accorded to the relations between them. Whether the problem concerns the environment, health, education, development or energy, and whether it is approached from a local, regional, national or universal standpoint, every time we find an abundance of approaches and areas of knowledge whose application is always perilous whether for research or for teaching purposes. The moment that universities organise their activities in accordance with *their function* and not the disciplines they teach, interdisciplinarity ceases to be a mere teaching device or the dream of certain enquiring minds and becomes an organisational need.

The work done by CERI on environmental education at university and post-secondary levels from 1971 to 1974 confirms this standpoint. In the conclusions to the Colloquium of Tours (France) in 1971 [40] we read:

"Since it breaks new ground on every count, environmental education means that knowledge must be reorganised in terms of present problems and the needs of the community. This calls for the revision of curricula, teaching methods and university structures, regarding all of which much remains to be discussed and much has yet to be done."

At the Colloquium in Rungsted (Denmark) in 1974 [41], Edward Wiedner, Chancellor of the University of Wisconsin-Green Bay put forward the following views in his opening address:

"Traditionally, the classical university has tried to remain aloof from society. It has been a retreat, a philosophical mecca. It has been based on the somewhat luxurious notion that society should provide a cloister for thinking. During their period of residence at a university students have been expected to remove themselves from society. While the classical university has accomplished far more than debate on how many angles could dance on the point of a pin it has emphasized knowledge for knowledge's sake, disciplinary learning for the discipline's sake, professional knowledge for the profession's sake and autonomy for the rest of society. Today the needs are for the university that is more fully a part of society even while retaining its autonomy and academic freedom. The needs are for a university that has a sense of social responsibility, that has a problem orientation to its curriculum, that is concerned with future time and that seeks the integration of knowledge."

The thinking that we did at the same time in the health training and research fields was an attempt to catch the conventional approach on the wrong foot. Instead of asking how interdisciplinarity should be developed in curricula, questions were put in a series like this. What is health? How should training be continually adapted to health requirements? What would be the optimum operational level for keeping the supply of health training abreast of demand in health matters? Interestingly, the implications for curricula and research programmes of a endogenous and an exogenous interdisciplinary approach can be highly different.

2. CHANGES IN INTERDISCIPLINARY CONTENT

The following practical example regarding new interdisciplinary curricula for medical staff will illustrate these changes.

In several countries there are medical faculties that have made far-reaching innovations by basing their training programmes on local public health and care requirements. Examples are Newcastle University in Australia, McMaster University in Canada, Negev University in Israel, University of Limburg in the Netherlands and the Metropolitan Autonomous University of Mexico. All of these have introduced interdisciplinary curricula based on community requirements. The following example shows how the State University of Limburg, Maastricht, in the Netherlands has organised its curricula. When the university was set up 1974 it defined its objectives as follows:

- To improve health care in the region by active participation in every aspect of health care;
- To create an integrated structure consisting of a regional medical centre (MRC) and the University of Maastricht Faculty of Medicine (MFM);
- To improve regional health education and health care by providing opportunities for training and research.

In 1977 the University made the latter objectives more specific:

- To organise an integrated programme of self-directed learning for medical students;
- To organise research as an integrated effort directed at a limited number of well-defined topics of importance for the further development of health care;
- To establish relationships between the university and the health care system of the region so that the potential of the University can be used for health care development and the health care system can provide varied clinical experience for medical students;
- To assist in the development of educational programmes for related health professions and eventually to integrate these programmes in a regional health university;
- To implement educational and health care research directed at the realisation and further development of the two above objectives.

It is clear that these objectives are in line with the new health responsibilities which the University of Limburg has undertaken in the region where it operates. It is interesting to note that the unifying subjects for teaching will be decided outside any epistemological or synthesis-oriented considerations. Here we are definitely dealing with exogenous interdisciplinarity based on observation of the actual health problems of individuals in the community. The curriculum for the first four years is organised as follows:

First year

Teaching unit	1.1	Introduction to medical studies
	1.2	Organisation and functioning of health care
	1.3	Accidental injuries
	1.4	Introduction to primary care
	1.5	Atherosclerosis
	1.6	Evaluation
	1.7	Infections and tumours – Introduction to clinical medicine.

Second year

Teaching unit	2.1	Embryo and foetus
	2.2.	The child
	2.3	The adolescent
	2.4	The adult
	2.5	The aged adult
	2.6	Evaluation
	2.7	Optional subjects

Third year

Teaching unit	3.1	Fatigue
	3.2	Life styles
	3.3.	Fevers and infections
	3.4	Shortness of breath and pain in the chest
	3.5	Bleeding
	3.6	Evaluation

Fourth year

Teaching unit	4.1	Abdominal complaints
	4.2	Menstrual disorders and complications of pregnancy
	4.3	Headache from the neurological and psychiatric standpoints
	4.4/4.5	Optional subjects
	4.6	Evaluation
	4.7	Pain in the back and in the arms and legs.

In the first year, for example, one of the unifying subjects (actually we should now revert to the term "problem" rather than "subject") is atherosclerosis. In the following matrix it can be seen that the disciplines involved in the analysis and solution of this problem are very diverse and not confined to the fundamental disciplines of natural science.

Myocardial infraction

Disciplines	Topics				
	First help	Physiology and anatomy of the heart	Therapy	Psychology of patients with pacemakers	Epidemiology of heart diseases
General medicine	**	*	**	*	*
Psychology			*	**	*
Sociology					**
Physiology	*	**	*		
Anatomy	*	**	*		
etc.					

*   Minor contribution.
** Major contribution.

	Myocardial infection	Cerebrovascular accident	Claudication
Biochemistry	***	**	**
Pharmacology	**	**	*
Physiology	***	***	**
Health economics	**	**	*
Internal medecine	**	**	**
Medical psychology	***	**	*
Morphology	***	**	**
Pathology	***	***	***
Laboratory work	***	**	***
Surgery	**	**	**
General medicine	***	***	***
First aid	***	**	*

*   No contribution.
**   Minor contribution to the problem in question.
*** Major contribution to the problem in question.

    These interdisciplinary curricula based on an analysis of real-life situations in the community seem to us conducive to a better matching of part of training and research to the health requirements of the community.

    A parallel example is provided by the *objectives and curricula of the University of Hacettepe in Turkey,*which is different from conventional medical universities in that the teaching there is based on interdisciplinarity. The following is a brief description.

    There are over 8 000 students at this University which was set up in 1967. The University is almost wholly geared to the training of health staff (full-length courses and short courses for paramedical and auxiliary health personnel).

    Its objectives may be defined as follows:

– To train health practitioners familiar with basic disciplines and the links connecting them in a university specialising in health education;
– To establish an integrated medical education system.

The integration objective is central to the experiment... "the teaching system is an integrated one, avoiding repetition and inviting dialogue between the various schools. The integrated teaching approach is one of the main features of the University of Hecettepe. The integrated teaching method covers the fundamental sciences, basic medical sciences and clinical instruction. The teaching programme was designed to facilitate integrated learning. During the first year in the faculty of medicine, basic sciences such as chemistry, physics, mathematics, molecular biology and the social sciences are integrated with each other and with community medicine. During the second year, 14 hours of theoretical teaching every week are devoted to an introduction to clinical sciences and community medicine (two hours of lectures and two hours of work in discussion groups). During the third year, students follow courses in the basic medical sciences such as microbiology, pharmacology and pathology. This part of the course is also integrated. The disciplines are taught by teachers from various institutes" [28].

This type of integration is a way of avoiding the traditional pluridisciplinarity of medical education which does not help a student in the synthesis that has to be made of the different subjects. The University of Hacetepe therefore decided to organise its curricula by basing the integration in the third year on the diseases of the major systems of the body which thus act as unifying subjects for various disciplines:

Third year (Course from 1967 to 1973)   *Weeks*

Mechanisms of cellular and tissue injury   4
Infectious diseases   7
Diseases of the cardiovascular and respiratory systems   4
Diseases of the digestive and hemotopoietic systems   5
Diseases of the endocrine and reproduction systems   4
Diseases of the urinary system   3
Diseases of the nervous system and psychiatry   4
Diseases of the muscular-skeletal system   3

The University of Hacettepe is a good example of *the transition from "exogenous" to "indogenous" interdisciplinarity,* because now the integration is more via pathologies than via the systems of the human body. It should also be noted that this remodelling of the curricula since 1973 was the direct result of the definition of new objectives which were: development of community medicine, emphasis on primary care, prevention and health education, approach to the individual's health problems from all three physical, mental and social standpoints and participation in the analysis of health requirements and the application of solutions.

3. INTERDISCIPLINARITY AND THE UNIVERSITY'S INSTITUTIONAL STRUCTURE

Various university structures are conceivable as a way of developing the kind of interdisciplinarity enabling a response to be made to the community's problems. We encountered many of these structures in the survey made in 1969 on interdisciplinarity experiments and in the survey carried out between 1976 and 1978. It must at once be pointed out that interdisciplinarity implies a *de facto* monodisciplinarity and that consequently there is no question of abolishing monodisciplinary departments. Instead the object is to develop institutional mechanisms enabling a different approach to be taken either the whole time or occasionally.

We were able to observe three types of institutional responses in the implementation of interdisciplinarity training or research activities:

- "Groups" (teaching staff, students, bodies representing the community concerned) set up to carry out a specific fixed-term project and therefore constituting a non-permanent institution;
- Interdisciplinary departments or schools set up to study certain problems (transport, urban planning, environment, energy, telecommunications, etc.). These departments are of necessity linked to the university's monodisciplinary departments;
- Whole universities set up for or geared to a problem of major social and economic importance such as technology, environment, health, etc.

The latter is a very ambitious and relatively original concept which is described in what follows.

Towards a regional interdisciplinary problem-oriented post-secondary structure

Earlier CERI work concerning education and research in the environment and health fields showed that new institutional structures of education were possible. There follows a description of a kind of model that is not exclusive of others.

Firstly it is a matter of developing a *post-secondary educational structure* with the following objectives:

- To allow better student guidance, and in that way to reduce the cost – and the frustrations – of failed leavers;
- To facilitate mobility of students in short (generally technical) cycles to the longer courses and vice versa; to develop common-core educational opportunities;
- To turn human and material resources to maximum account;
- To offer a more flexible framwork for continuous and recurrent education; to develop links between education at various levels and research;
- Lastly, to allow diversification of responsibility at the various educational levels and institutions in relation to the demands made by the surrounding communities. The third cycle research level, for example, may be required to analyse a requirement and the short-cycle course level to put this or that solution into effect.

The unifying element or elements both inside the university and in its relation with the community then become structures oriented towards *the study of one or more problems*. The choice of problems must be sufficiently wide so as to promote to the maximum a concerted and integrated approach involving the various disciplines and sufficiently practical to be recognised immediately by the surrounding communities. Examples are energy, transport, urban planning, technology, the environment and health. If the problem leads on to highly varied professions, research at the heterogeneous level and direct action in the community itself, a post-secondary structure needs to be set up wholly and exclusively for the subject. There are fairly numerous examples of "universities" or university centres (combining long and short-cycle courses, fundamental research and applied research) focused on technology, health or the environment. It is important to note that all these institutions by the very nature of the subject chosen give practically equal – or almost equal – importance to natural and human sciences.

This model is indeed *of the interdisciplinary type because it is based on a pluri-dimensional approach. In it there is to be found the combination of two types of institution :*

Specialised and generally mono-disciplinary institutions

Their mission will be to maintain and develop each special discipline. They will need to be responsible for training their specialists, developing their specific technology and endeavouring to apply in-depth analysis to the phenomena observed from their various sources of study.

Such institutions will not have the task of defining their field of action in isolation except for the most fundamental parts of their theoretical and technological teaching. Basically, they are not involved in the training of students.

Interdisciplinary problem-oriented institutions

These institutions will develop their training and research in a specific field in response to the requirements of the region in which they operate. Examples are health and the environment, the development and organisation of production, etc. Their function will not be to develop special disciplines but to conduct a permanent and as exhaustive as possible an analysis of the fields for which they are responsible. Their particular task will be to define the training required to meet the specific needs of the region and they will therefore need to supply an adequate number of specialists of the relevant quality.

These institutions will also be a special forum for discussing the divergent interests of organised groups or individuals, analysing problems and proposing solutions. They will be centres for consultation, investigation and experiment and will maintain close and permanent contacts with actual development in the fields of study concerned.

The "post-secondary complex will initially be defined by the problems concerned and the regions in which action is to be taken.

For this purpose, various combinations of monodisciplinary institutions and interdisciplinary problem-oriented institutions can be envisaged. The "regional problem-oriented university" may associate one or more problem-oriented institutions just as a monodisciplinary institution may be associated with one or more "regional problem-oriented universities".

The problem-oriented institutions will in most cases be the parent units for structures and facilities for action in the region, for the university and the local community will co-operate exclusively through the bodies they have set up for guidance and management and it will then become possible to decide simultaneously what training and research can be assigned more especially to conventional academic staff and in what training projects and research community leaders will co-operate with teachers and students "in the field".

The optimum level for such a structure to operate seems to be the region. In Part One, Chapter 3, we saw that it was not possible systematically to identify community and region because the term may apply to administrative boundaries or to geographical, cultural or population characteristics. Nevertheless, the term is used deliberately here to define a kind of territorial responsibility for the problem-oriented post-secondary structure. The essential feature of the region is the minimum geographical demographic, cultural, economic and social unit required for recruiting students into the various curricula, capable of providing jobs for the various types of graduate and sufficiently large to promote a productive symbiotic relationship between the community and the university's training and research facilities. This minimum varies widely, depending on population density, transport facilities and natural obstacles, language barriers, degree of industrialisation and the economic level of the region concerned.

136

The "region" is therefore the best level of community for this type of structure because it means that:

- Optimum use can be made of the resources of higher education structures and the resources of the community (human, material and infrastructure resources);
- Closer relationships can be established between higher education and economic and cultural activities, in particular employment, and an efficient system of alternation can be set up;
- Participation in the search for cultural and individual identity based on regional characteristics can be effectively pursued;
- Easier access is possible to higher education for the various socio-economic groups in the community; teaching "in the field" is possible;
- A sustained effort can be pursued to make training and research consistent with the needs felt by the population;
- Higher education can contribute to regional development policies.

CONCLUSION

Interdisciplinarity is both the basis and stumbling block of education that rests on the development of relations with the community. It may be purely theoretical, purely artificial, representing the unrealised dream of a kind of total knowledge cherished by every university man.

In many experiments, it is certainly the product of personal interest (or the friendly relations of certain teachers and scientists) or the endogenous development of the requirements of scientific knowledge. But interdisciplinarity may also be something extremely concrete and very precise when it comes from outside, in other words when it corresponds to the effective complexity and "multi-referential" character of all real problems. It would seem, moreover, that the communities – through their increased demand for assistance in analysing and solving their social and economic problems – may be in a position to force the university to completely remodel its curricula and research programmes and its institutional structures. Inter-disciplinary curricula and research programmes thus tend to build themselves up around the requests from the community, and institutional structures tend to develop along lines – particularly in the case of a regional interdisciplinary problem-oriented post-secondary structure – which make the university socially more responsible to the regional community. This trend, however, is taking place only very slowly and certainly not universally.

The reason why university structures organised on the pattern of monodisciplinary departments are rigid is because disciplines are not simply scientific realities but also social institutions which define a sharing of knowledge or of power. This is clear from the way in which research committees tend to share out and divide up the various tasks proposed to them and try to enclose them within disciplinary frameworks which are at the same time frameworks of budgetary appropriations and power.

In that connection, the following chapter describes the specific aspects of interdisciplinary research in the university-community relationship.

It is tempting to conclude this chapter with the words of Eric Jantsch who, in the 1970 OECD Seminar on Interdisciplinarity, had already seen this role of interdisciplinarity perfectly clearly as a factor of change in the missions of the university when he said:

137

"The task of turning the university from a passive servant of various elements of society and of individual and even egoistic ambitions of the members of its community into an active institution participating in the process of planning for society implies profound changes in purpose and thought, as well as in institutional and individual behaviour. It will give the university freedom, dignity, and significance – qualities which have become distorted in a process in which the university is used, but is not expected and not permitted to participate actively. The thorny path to an inter- and transdisciplinary university has been outlined in my paper as the way for the university to assume a new and active role in society." [39]

Chapter 3

RECONCILING THE REQUIREMENTS OF RESEARCH AND THOSE OF THE COMMUNITY

There can hardly be any denying that a certain unrest is affecting the world of university research. The participation of scientists in protests, ideological and political movements and the great number of colloquies and other conferences on the role of research are both evidence of a certain crumbling of the system in which research and the university research worker quite naturally fitted, the former as a necessary contributor to progress in economic and social well-being and the latter as the guarantor of that progress, a symbolic figure at the opening of the twentieth century in the same way as the teacher only more so. This unrest in research but also the resolve of research to assert its necessity and specificity are not unrelated to the socio-economic and institutional context, in which the position and status of university research seem, at least in the eyes of those mainly concerned, to have continually deteriorated particularly over the last ten years.

A first feature of this context stems from the fact that an increasingly large part of research work is undertaken outside university circles proper, namely in the framework of public, semi-public or private sector centres, thus outside the control of university scientists. In France, for example, the Commissariat à l'Énergie atomique (CEA), Électricité de France (EDF), the Institut de la Santé et de la Recherche Médicale (INSERM), and the Institut Pasteur are examples of non-university institutions making a highly significant contribution to research. The same applies in other countries; in the United States, for example, there is NASA, the Jet Propulsion Laboratory and, of course, all the research laboratories of the big firms like Bell, IBM, etc. True, in most cases, these non-university research institutions have developed close links with the university. The fact remains that the university – in such essential fields as atomic science, molecular biology, energy, and so on – would seem to be increasingly ousted from control over research and, losing the initiative, relegated to a subsidiary role. This is probably a reason for the relative marginalisation of the university research scientist.

The phenomenon is all the more marked in that the financing of research itself has undergone radical changes in its structure and in funding procedures.

- The components of external finance, in other words that which is added to universities' own research finance, have changed considerably. In terms of percentage of aggregate finance, external funding has remained at a stable level over the last ten years (though the level varies from country to country [42]: 40 per cent in Canada, 18 per cent in Australia, 26 per cent in Switzerland, etc.). But whereas regular sources (foundations, trusts, etc.) have gone down, grants from governments (and government agencies) and from the industrial sector have increased. These supplementary resources – often vital just to keep the budgets of the beneficiary institutions in balance – are not general grants which the universities are free to dispose of as they will but are allocated on the basis of research (and often R&D) programmes whose objects, like the yardsticks for allocation, are largely outside the universities' control;

- A similar phenomenon, bound up with the growing dependence on outside resources, is at work at the level of the decision-making structures. Not only has the relative weight of external finance (which is project-linked and no longer institution-based) been increasing but at the same time, as a logical consequence of this, the chains of decision have become longer and heavier. In other words, support from the government has become bureaucratised (with more and more committees, commissions and other government offices responsible for managing the decision-making process). Here again it may be wondered whether this phenomenon is not also partly responsible for the unrest referred to above (and for the – almost reactionary – insistence of university scientists on asserting their independence and specificity, a subject to which we shall return later on).

A second factor to be borne in mind seems to us to be purely and simply the effects of a considerable increase in the university student population – at least up to 1975, because the available statistics point to more or less zero growth thereafter except in some countries like Greece and also Japan. These effects are of various kinds.

- An increase in university staff and, given the fact that financial resources have not in general kept pace with inflation, a parallel and relative decrease in the amounts available for university research (after meeting the wage bill and the costs of teaching materials);
- A significant corresponding increase in the number of research-students (third-cycle students) particularly, in the opinion of some, as in the field of the human sciences in particular, this may be a kind of bridging situation for some students because of the difficulties of finding jobs. The figures collected by the OECD for Sweden, for example, lead to the curious conclusion that whilst the number of doctorate students increased by an average of 41 per cent in 1979 compared with 1978 (94 per cent in medicine, 42 per cent in the arts, 5 per cent in natural sciences, etc.) the number of doctorates actually conferred went down (except in the case of medicine).

The fact that an increasingly large number of students (including third-cycle students) contrasts with decreasing research appropriations (in relative terms) inevitably affects the status of university research.

On top of all these phenomena there is another and equally important development, namely the fact that university research is increasingly costly. The number of research fields not requiring the use of the computer and other electronic equipment – from linguistics to medical research – is steadily shrinking. Sampling and data collection formulae are increasingly complex and, in all countries, a basic requirement is to keep up to date, to be in touch with what other scientists are doing and to exchange experience. All these features of research – in particular, but not only, university research – mean high additional unit costs both at the staff level (technicians, documentalists, etc.) and in hardware. The difficulty universities have in financing these costs out of own funds and therefore the internal and external pressures they are under to find other resources are certainly not calculated to strengthen the conviction of the university scientist. Whilst they may cause him to assert all the more the irreducible nature of his position, they help, in so doing, to accentuate his isolation.

1. AN OUTDATED ISSUE

It is in this context that, seeking the better to identify possible lines along which co-operation between the university and its environment might be intensified, we need to return to the old issue of the nature of university research itself (by contrast with a type of research, which would be more directly geared to the immediate requirements of a particular group of people commissioning the research such as the government, industry, regional authorities, etc.). Is the contrast that between "pure", "theoretical" and "fundamental" research and applied, practical (or technological) and impure research? This is a field full of trip wires which, above all, seems to us to reflect, if anything, a somewhat traditional and idealistic system of representing the university. The terms put forward by university people themselves to describe their research institutions tend to highlight the autonomous character of research, stripped of any utilitarian aims (social, economic, monetary, etc.). It goes without saying in this perspective that from the researchers' viewpoint *pure research is good research,* escaping by definition from any political dependence and in no danger of serving the purposes of factions, evil and debatable forces or economic interests. The fundamental researcher is both untrammelled and faultless. Even when university students or teachers engage in contemporary political struggles, they tend to do so in the name of the independence of science and its non-submission to economic imperatives. Everyone is aware that the events at Berkeley University in the United States in 1964 – the first incident in the worldwide wave of student protest that followed – were very strongly linked to questioning about the role of science as well as all the demonstrations against the Vietnam war.

Paradoxically, and according to circumstances, *some therefore appeal to the independence of university research as the basis of a political stance, and others to the necessary neutrality of the university in order to subordinate research more to the immediate aims of society.*

This seems to us to be a false debate or rather a false dilemma. The opposition – or pseudo-opposition – between fundamental and applied research has many forms and does not stand up very well to even an elementary semantic analysis.

On the one hand, stress is laid on fundamental science, regarded as a body of primary knowledge, on which the applied sciences derived from it are based, but very quickly a second acceptation takes over with fundamental science being what is most important or essential by contrast to what is secondary. If the former distinction is scientifically analysable, the latter is purely ideological and socially dependent.

On the other, fundamental research is contrasted with applied research in terms of what is universal versus what is particular and specific. This contradistinction reflects the hierarchy in international, national and regional functions. Universities are regarded as having, by definition, an international vocation with their staff (the researchers) having no accounts to render except to their peers. Their location is not their particular environment, it is all the other universities with whom they feel a common bond and to which their work is addressed. Only applied research is expected to give an account of what it does to a specific environment.

Yet a further school of thought identifies fundamental with advanced research. The purpose of the university is to produce new knowledge, open up new fields and to enable mankind to progress. Applied research would be the exploitation of that advanced research. It is therefore, by definition, one step behind. It aims at well-being and efficiency and may relate, without distinction, to interests in industry, in the economy, in the community, etc.

The university's function in fundamental research, therefore, is, as it were, the reverse of its privileged status; it expresses a kind of social division of scientific labour. Applied research is a matter for business, the community and specialised laboratories. Admittedly, a research assignment may well be submitted to a university by its environment but the idea is to utilise available intellectual and technical resources and, ultimately, to use any additional funds that the assignment may bring with it to increase opportunities for pursuing the university's own research which can only be fundamental. Here, once more, we find service defined as a secondary and superficial activity that makes no change to the more fundamental vocation of the higher education system.

Choosing fundamental research as one's proper subject therefore implies both increasing one's worth at the ideological level and freeing oneself from the hobbling constraints that research directed towards practical purposes implies, namely maintaining links with all the production structures, getting to know their concrete problems and keeping oneself informed of the effective value of the solutions proposed and their real-life application. Every influence therefore acts in the direction of keeping the system in its most traditional and debatable form.

Clearly, and it has to be realised, reality is completely different. Far from being centres of excellence, the universities and the research departments within them are no longer purely the business of an "élite" of the population and even less a student-élite. The considerable growth of higher education establismments outside the universities (the "grandes écoles" in France, the MIT and Caltech in the United States are examples) and their prestige and power of attraction have thoroughly demolished this somewhat élitist conception of the university. It even looks as though the democratisation of secondary education has, as it were, strengthened a movement in the reverse direction; it is precisely these extra-university establishments that now enjoy a high reputation, attract the "best" students and pull towards them large-scale external resources. This view admittedly needs closer definition. It is mainly in the scientific and technological fields and, more generally, in those fields that have immediate economic and social utility that these extra-university establishments are the most developed, leaving the universities to some extent the less directly utilitarian, some would say more "theoretical", fields.

What is more, constantly proclaiming the precedence of theory over practice, of the general over the particular, university scientists (and officials) tend to forget that research – even the most fundamental research – must sooner or later find some social link. Rather, the extraordinary growth of knowledge, the fact that it is increasingly impossible to isolate research fields from one another and the fine division and high specialisation of the very object of research, in other words the internal and external requirements of research dynamics increase the need to associate the "pure" with the "impure" the "theoretical" with the "practical", the "fundamental" with the "applied". And all the more so in that there is no social progress that does not show evidence of this to-and-fro movement in which simultaneously all technologies, in other words all applied sciences, reflect the social integration of the scientific activity concerned and where the latter itself finds the deep-lying reasons for its existence in the ambition to solve concrete problems.

The idea we discussed in the previous chapter that concepts like health and environment are *central and fundamental* and that they serve as a basis for understanding problems peculiar to each discipline is therefore tantamount not only to pursuing another model for the relations between science and the community but also to reversing the traditional problems of science. In a word, the relationship to application is not a simple relationship. It is not the mere projection, onto a complex reality, of exact knowledge obtained via the fundamental sciences. As a director at the Technical University of Berlin points out, this involves an inevitable and positive conflict of values: "the conflict exists but it is inherent in the system and therefore must be considered as a productive conflict between two positions of equal value, i.e. theory and practice. In this sense, applied research may be considered to be part of a recurrent cycle".

What is important is to get away from a purely linear conception. Even if the picture is complicated by bringing in oriented research and research and development, the main problem is not only to juxtapose the terms and refine the definition of distinct categories but to show the way the different levels interact.

University research generally proceeds from a theoretical problem connected with the development of knowledge and techniques of research itself. Each specialist considers that practice is the field of application of the general laws stated by his discipline. Application is then seen as secondary fall-out, willingly left to specialised institutions or fims. But cannot applied research be regarded as part of a feedback system enriching and, at the same time, relativising specialised thinking? Cannot research into community needs and problems be included in this recurrent cycle of pure and applied research?

If we respond to the needs of the community by problem-oriented or mission-oriented research, can we not transform this relationship which is univocal at the outset into a bi-univocal relationship of such a nature that it enriches specialised knowledge? There are certainly many examples of research on a given problem which have sometimes led to spectacular advances in fundamental research. The study of certain diseases, for example, has brought considerable progress in many scientific disciplines. In the other direction, advances in specialised knowledge have led to more effective insight into certain areas of pathology and their treatment.

Moreover, this critical analysis could be extended by asking the question whether the apparent debate within the "theoretical or fundamental research/applied research" pair does not, instead, reflect an objective alliance in which different actors often fulfil themselves. In other words, there could be a kind of "complicity" between the university and the social system: society reproaches university research for turning away from social concerns and pursuing knowledge for its own sake but at the same time it prefers things to be as they are because the aloofness of the scientist allows society to reject any scientific criticism of the way it functions. Need it be said in this connection, as already pointed out, that far from revolting against this situation, university research is to a large extent ready to play along because, in doing so, its (apparent) "independence" is further strengthened?

The logic is even stronger when the critical power of the universities (and research scientists in particular) expresses itself outside the university. It is not by chance, for example, that ecological and antinuclear movements have been strongly supported by scientists who would here seem to have found a channel through which they can express their rejection of a technocratic and utilitarian society and at the same time affirm their legitimacy as scientists. Is it any surprise, too, to see so many university researchers interested in phenomena of social and in particular urban disintegration, the result of economic growth taken to the extreme, whereas they have seen their role, power and status so emphatically marginalised by this growth? Without wishing to caricaturise this tendency, it might be said that the poor relations of the system of research and development – university research and research scientists – have tried, by affirming the specificity and legitimacy of their relative isolation, to counterbalance the latter by defending the victims of growth and by recapturing, in so doing, some social status.

2. MAIN LINES OF A NEW RELATIONSHIP BETWEEN UNIVERSITY RESEARCH AND ITS ENVIRONMENT, THE SOCIO-ECONOMIC CONTEXT

It is not possible to define (or redefine) the problems of the relationships between university research and its environment without, at the outset, taking the new situation and the new issues of the socio-economic context into account. Clearly, the development of science and technology is intimately bound up with and influenced by economic growth. As has been rightly pointed out in a recent OECD publication [43] it is important "to maintain and improve the innovative capacity and to exploit this capacity to sustain a high rate of technical advance and productivity increase throughout the economy and particularly to help in solving urgent problems of energy-saving and energy supply".

This correlation between productivity gain (bound up with technological innovation) in a given sector of production and relative price stability in the same sector (as for electrical household appliances and textiles) goes hand in hand with another phenomenon which cannot fail to be worrying for the future of university research, namely the more or less steady decline in industrial investment in long-term research on minor improvements in products and processes which intensify the substitution of capital for labour and ultimately increase the level of unemployment.

This, therefore, is the context – slower growth in productivity accompanied by high rates of unemployment and inflation – in which we have to place the problems of university research and, more generally, the role of research within the universities in the framework of their interrelations with their environment.

A central theme of this new statement of problems could be this: it is in the field of what some authors have called "strategic" research – "in other words research that concerns neither problems of immediate utility, nor problems in which the only interest is scientific theory" [42] – that university research (bearing in mind the reluctance of industry to invest in R&D on the development of fundamental technologies, the only ones capable of creating jobs in sufficent number) is able to make a significantly large contribution to improving innovation capability. The term "fundamental technology" should here be understood in its widest sense, namely "technologies" whose achievements depend on medium and, sometimes, long-term research that may appear to be too applied in the eyes of traditional universities and too hazardous or ill-defined in the eyes of industry (mainly concerned with immediate return), but which nevertheless bring forth industrial innovations whose economic and social consequences may be considerable."

It would, in fact, be wrong to limit this new statement of the unversity research problem purely to industrial technologies however fundamental they may be. All "social" technologies are also concerned, in other words those concerning community products and services for which – however implicit it may be by comparison with personal consumer goods – the (social) demand is increasingly in evidence. To the extent that one of the essential yardsticks for community goods is that of the quality of their distribution in society, it would therefore be crucial, following the logic of the above, that university research should be closely involved in analysing mechanisms for the diffusion of these community goods.

A second thrust which, in its case too, would help to find a way out of the classic opposition between applied and fundamental research, is that of what we shall call "public service" research, based directly on the immediate and future needs of individuals and communities. This, therefore, finds its source in the reality of the increasingly complex situations that society is faced with. This is the sense in which it would be a public service. Whether it be called mission-oriented, public-oriented, public service or active research, its definition is difficult if the traditional yardsticks are used and the same ambiguity that we discussed in Part One in relation to the concept of service again applies. The University of California, for example, points out that "Public service research has proved even more difficult to measure than applied research, no doubt in part because it is not a usual funding category. In one sense, all official activity, including research, in a public university is public service; in another, only items that appear in the accounting system under "public service" or "extension" would qualify. We have adopted a working definition somewhere in between: public service research is that part of the university's applied research effort that is intended to assist some public, or an agency representing public, interests" [9].

The characteristic of this type of research is that it is now almost always pluridisciplinary, corresponding to the demand and needs of the community, and this pluridisciplinarity cuts across the natural and human sciences. Tackling the energy problem is no longer just a matter of fundamental research on nuclear fission and fusion. Some countries are in difficulties because they have failed to deal with this problem in the framework of the social sciences as well. In our industrialised countries, any research on the diseases which affect the individual as such and in his environment necessarily involves a combination of biomedical research and medico-social research.

The "public service" research projects based on this combination of natural and human sciences are numerous and always very difficult to put into effect for the following reasons:

- The generally monodisciplinary structure of research units in higher education institutions. They have not known how to keep pace with the increase in knowledge. Many special disciplines have had to split off and form new specialist branches. They are all fearful of losing their specific characteristics if they form an association. Whether they are afraid of disappearing or are striving to assert themselves, they are all institutionalised in isolated structures.
- The trend of public service research towards institutionalisation in a separate structure: rejected by traditional university institutions, activities developed for the benefit of the community have very often been grouped together in an autonomous structure annexed to the parent institution (see Part Two, Chapter 2). Interdisciplinary public service research needs to draw its nourishment from specialised departments. It calls on the aid of researchers who do not necessarily belong to the parent institution and this leads to a regrettable underemployment of resources.
- To this must be added the fact, as pointed out by Arthur Brownlea at the February 1980 Conference, that a priority problem does not always represent a research priority and that a research priority may not be a priority in terms of service to the community. In any case the outlooks – even though they may complement each other, are different. It is difficult to find a balance between long-term theoretical research and the need for rapid progress at the practical level (e.g. between work on the etiology of cancer and the effectiveness of breast cancer early-warning methods). Structural arrangements may help to improve communication between researchers and decision-makers but they are inadequate and in any case the outcome of the problem largely depends on the main protagonists, the scale of the resources utilised in research, the effectiveness of the pressure groups and the credibility of the arguments (sometimes contradictory) put forward on either side.

It is from the same standpoint that the contribution of the university (and therefore of university research) to the development of community knowledge and of soft or light technology may be regarded, potentially, as most significant. These two possible sectors of activity have in common the fact that they both largely stem from daily life and therefore, in so doing, intimately affect the integration of the university in its economic and social environment. Just as the university can and should play an important part in the initial and continuous training of the bringers of change (apart from students, therefore, the training of decision-makers in their environment) so it can and ought also to be active in the development of innovation in sectors which are still marked by too artisanal an approach.

Solutions to the problems facing the individual and the community could be found by the use of empirical knowledge likely to place formal knowledge in a relative light and here, too, feedback between "practice" and "fundamental research" should be established. Indeed the essential problem is whether or not higher education is willing to accept the intrusion of a form of knowledge which does not obey the rules governing the production of academic knowledge which may well challenge but also enrich and supplement it. The example of acupuncture, which goes back 6 000 years, is significant in this respect. It is possible to treat a number of pathological states on the strength of a body of empirical knowledge which is not based on the organisation of our traditional medical knowledge. But, as we know, it is difficult to secure recognition for this empirical knowledge in the medical faculties of certain countries. There are numerous examples of this form of knowledge possessed by the community but rejected by scientific circles. In some countries, there is an awareness of the rich resources at the disposal of the community. Students of psychiatry in the faculty of medicine at Dakar (Senegal), for example, are observing and striving to understand exorcism, spontaneous psycho-drama and group dynamics etc. in African villages. In exchange they are making their traditional biochemical knowledge available to the community. In other words, empirical knowledge must be used more fully than before as a stimulus to theoretical research and much less often as a cover to prove that a given theory is true.

This rehabilitation of empirical knowledge long spurned by the university is not a return to pre-scientific attitudes but part of the recognition of a brutal fact, namely that research exists only in the most developed fields. It has been said that 10 per cent of a country's activity absorbs 90 per cent of its research. The consequences are paradoxical. Industrialised societies can develop highly advanced technologies but their day-to-day behaviour has remained at the pre-logical level. They are capable of computing the trajectory of a rocket but incapable of calculating the optimum level of heating or air conditioning.

In other words, as a result of the privileges granted to certain advanced technologies which have developed for historical or cultural reasons, there are whole sectors of human behaviour which are outside the scientific approach. An approach which takes empirical social practice into account is therefore not at all unscientific but, on the contrary, promotes the application of rational thought and criticism to sectors which have so far tended to restrict its field of application. When F. Meyer-Alich, of the University of Essen, speaks of the "socialisation of nature" in his study, he is advocating an enlargement of scientific method and not simply a sentimental reconciliation between man and his environment or traditions. Consequently, when the community hopes that research can be applied to practical areas where there are no established theories or definite experiments with established systems of concept, this does not mean that scientific research should be deviated from its course but that the field of rational thinking should be extended. It is understandable that this should be repugnant to scientists for they will lose their privileges and their certitudes. It is also understandable that local authorities, whether institutions or leading citizens, will often reject such intervention by the institutions of higher education. In both cases it is because what is at stake is the critical function of science.

3. THE EMERGENCE OF NEW PARTNERS: CONFLICTS AND NEW TRENDS

What has just been said widens the issue. If the requirements of research and demand from the community are to be reconciled this means, not only at the outset but throughout the whole process, that the various people involved overcome their own inertia (including that at the level of representation) and be prepared for exchanges between them, the terms of which are certainly not predetermined. Better– or worse – even, an approach of this kind, and all the more so if it affects the "social" technologies field, cannot avoid bringing to the surface conflicts likely to strengthen defensive (or even "protectionist") attitudes, with the community unprepared to accept the idea that the university should interfere in "political" power and action and the university refusing to accept that the content and direction of its "research" should not be just as exclusively the province of the university.

The potential dangers – or occasions – of conflict would appear to be all the more implicit in an approach aimed at strengthening the interrelations between university research and its environment in that firstly the ground covered by these exchanges and secondly the partners involved are far from being immediately identifiable:

- By definition, the field where the two meet is primarily that of the problems encountered by the community, to the solution of which it is intended that university research should contribute. Over and above the contributions it already makes in answer to specific commissions from the industrial world (where the input from university research is basically technical), economic and social problems (under the headings or urban planning, social action, and so on) lead university research onto necessarily more political ground where the boundary between research and action is far more vague.
- Over and above the assignments from industry, mainly from the big industrial groups, the stronger links between a university and the community will bring new actors on the scene who, up to now, have had neither the resources nor the opportunity of putting in their requests (i.e. their problems): first and foremost the local communities, but also small and medium-sized firms, not forgetting groups of common interest with or without elective status. Developing co-operation with such varied partners will not be a very easy task for university research, particularly given present budgetary constraints. Here, one of the main obstacles seems to be the absence of a shared language.

   The big firms and, more generally, their senior staffs, and public officials are all university products. They know the institutional mechanisms of the university and share, more or less, their values and prejudices. They use the same concepts and the same methods. But relations with small- and medium-sized firms, local communities and various groups of citizens could well be no more than mistrust and a reciprocal lack of comprehension. Whence a vast area of major difficulties and misunderstandings.

It should not be believed, however, that the trends described above define a set of problems necessarily running counter to present trends. In fact, these new orientations are part of a context where new types of relationship between university and environment are already coming into being. There are several reasons why the changes suggested above might be regarded as perfectly possible.

Firstly, the constraints of universities' reduced financial resources, particularly for research, are, so to speak, forcing the institutions to look for outside support. Another fact to bear in mind is the effect of all the social pressures tending to make the university – including research – more responsible for and more relevant to the needs of the community (the American term "accountability" is an even better expression than "relevance" for this pressure on the universities to develop more socially responsible attitudes with regard to the considerable human and physical resources they are given).

Secondly, there is the movement towards greater interdisciplinarity, another contributory factor in this new dilemma. The movement is accentuated by the advent of a new student population – the adult students already in working life who, within their educational demands themselves, initiate this return to practice in research.

A last factor, more exogenous than the movement towards interdisciplinarity and the appearance of a new student population, is that of the dispersal and increasing number of university establishments. Although, at the national level, the criticisms of duplication of and in universities and sometimes wastage of resources might be warranted, the large number of units and their dispersed nature present an opportunity more particularly to "small" universities whose legitimacy can be all the more asserted if they develop close relations with their environment and, in so doing, become close relations with their environment and, in so doing, become a vital element in the definition of problems, the search for solutions and the implementation of the chosen action.

CONCLUSION

One would wish to conclude this chapter by insisting on the dynamic and conflictual nature of the university research situation. In the face of the internal and external – and sometimes contradictory – pressures upon it, research – and therefore university researchers – could yield to one of two temptations: to hide away in a kind of "scientific purity" and thus become isolated from the external world, counting on their "excellence" but also the privileged relations that they have with the nation's other "élites" to protect them from what they regard as a contamination of science, or else, wishing to be recognised by their peers but also by big industry and the State, to strive to strengthen their links with both by directing their teaching and research, for example, towards what is regarded as useful and effective by them but always from the same élitist angle that brings them to do battle with the "competition" – high-level non-university institutions. Neither of these two paths seems to us to offer much promise, beyond a short term future on which the universities have little direct graps.

A third path remains, narrow, difficult and uncertain, though it does not exclude so-called fundamental research nor contracts with big industry and the authorities. It is to be the locus of a critical, continuous and recurrent exchange between practice and theory based one on the other and where, incidentally, the social dimension would play the essential part. It is solely on this condition that, refusing doubtful loyalties and avoiding the dilemmas implicit in the title of this chapter, the university, and more particularly university research, will retain its full legitimacy.

Conclusion

FROM FREEDOM WITHOUT POWER TO PARTNERSHIP IN SOCIAL CHANGE

Of all the problems with which a policy for higher education must deal, the proper relationship between the universities and their environment is the one presenting the greatest diversity, whether at national and regional levels or at the level of a single institution. It should not be surprising, therefore that, despite the wide variety and intimacy of the situations and experiences here examined, we have been unable to read a set of conclusions that are both simple and of universal application.

We do not intend here to go back over the organisational, pedagogic and scientific consequences resulting from the development of those relationships. It is much more important to bring out the three major questions underlying the set of issues that we have tried to develop. These questions seem to us to require answers if the dynamic that we have been able to discern is not to remain simply a conjunctural phenomenon which will not bring about a positive redefinition of the university/community relationship. First, the increase in activities directed towards the community, the taking into account of new populations, the widening of the field of scientific interest are not enough in themselves to define a new policy. Second, the elaboration of global strategies and the introduction of a degree of "institutional transparency" are indispensable preliminaries. Third, there must be a clear understanding of what is meant by university autonomy. Without the answers to such questions this study would have finished up as a collection of disparate experiences – interesting enough, but of no real help in framing new university policies in a time of crisis.

1. TWO BASIC OBSERVATIONS

While it is itself a complex community, and while one is prepared to recognise that it has a number of objectives of its own, the university is everywhere considered as an integral part of the community and hence necessarily subject to a number of developments which are themselves determined by changes in society. The questions we have to consider therefore are how the contemporary university fits into the social fabric, how it reacts to the pressures exerted on it, how it creates the mechanisms that enable it to interrelate with the society around it, and what forms of activity it uses to intervene in that society. Whatever the solutions or approaches recommended, we have been able to observe that, as far as the functions of the university are concerned, two tendencies exist:

Maintenance of traditional activities.

The production of new knowledge and qualified students (with or without degrees) remains in the long term the major type of intervention by the university in the community. It is important therefore to maintain and develop the traditional functions of higher education, and in particular the provision of rigorous intellectual training. The various surveys have shown that, whatever the category of population interrogated, the first demand is for an individual education of high quality. *The university must therefore continue its teaching and research functions and exercise them to the full as services to the community.*

Emergence of new functions

We encountered a general consensus as to the desirability of the university and the community making their human and material resources available to each other. As pointed out by the German Conference of University Rectors: "the mutual exchange of equipment, infrastructural and human resources reflects a need which is felt both by the community and by the higher education institution". As to the adoption of this idea in all Member countries, however, the administrative, technical and human conditions for such exchanges would require means of implementation individually adapted to national and local situations. Nor could they be the same for public and private institutions, for example.

We also found that there was a similar consensus in favour of a recommendation that the university should enlarge the field of the partners it addresses:

- In the productive sector, it is asked to develop relations with small and medium-sized enterprises that do not possess their own facilities for research or training;
- In the public authorities field there has been enlargement in university relations with local authorities who, again, do not possess their own facilities for research or for the analysis of problems and monitoring solutions.
- In the social field the universities are increasingly addressing themselves to populations that have not hitherto had access to higher education. This they are doing by encouraging access of workers to higher education, by increasing continuing training activities and encouraging their interpenetration with "normal" education, and by addressing themselves to new populations "who do not know how to get to the university", such as ethnic or cultural minorities and old people. This improvement of access to the universities presupposes both a wider spread of higher education institutions and a change in conditions for entry so that occupational experience and other criteria may be taken into account.

Heterogeneity of the solutions

From the body of actual practices connected with the two points made above, it is possible to draw several consequences:

- The diversity among the solutions adopted stems directly from differences in national situations, in university traditions, and in the avowed objectives of higher education. Such diversity, far from being an obstacle to university/community relations, must be respected and maintained; but it must mean that no one solution can be recommended as a model for general application internationally – or nationally.
- One generalisation that can be made from the evidence is that the development of relations with the community does not depend solely on the goodwill of the

university, nor on the degree of autonomy it has to determine its own policy. It turns just as much on national policies and on the degree of autonomy possessed by the "outside" bodies with which the university co-operates, whether these be local or regional authorities, firms, trade unions or other kinds of associations. None of the university/community procedures we have examined can be considered as fully positive. We found, for example, that the multi-site universities, thoroughly immersed as they are in their respective communities, find it particularly difficult to define their own identity. In these cases, the reciprocal use of resources creates complicated problems for administrative and financial management and sometimes exacerbates conflict. Another valid generalisation is that the liaison structures most effective from the operational point of view tend to acquire their own autonomy and thus give succour to the university's inborn resistance to change. We have noted, too, that while the growing variety of sources of finance and possible centres of decision-making may result in an increase in global resources, it also tends towards a blurring of criteria of accountability.

- The approaches to university/community relations seem to result much more from a series of conjunctural events than from rational examination of what they involve. The general reduction in resources allocated to universities and hence the need to find other sources of finance is one example of this.

Up to the present, then, the increase in university/community relations can be seen as the product of a convergence of widely different approaches ranging from the promotion of a more democratic society to the concern to develop scientific research or the setting up of institutions offering higher returns. It has rarely been the result of more systematic thinking about the ultimate purposes of universities or the optimal practical conditions for achieving them. As already observed, there is an inevitability about the heterogeneity of the objectives pursued in the course of university/community relations and there is no point in trying to reduce it. If, however, we are to consider practical measures to attain them, *this must be done within wider strategies, that would embrace them all.* This applies particularly to an observable reluctance to make a final choice between central policies of financial aids and legislation linked with the desire for a planned development, to purely empirical practices of alternation and exchange of personnel, and to management policies, both more democratic and more operational, that are based on participation mechanisms. This is why we have tried (in particular in Chapter 4 of Part One) to identify these various strategies as clearly as possible, not in order to express a preference for any particular one but to reveal possible conflicts and contradictions.

2. TOWARDS GLOBAL STRATEGIES

In our view there are three basic factors in any global strategy for the development of university/community relations: the regional dimension, a two-way flow of information, and planned changes in policies for post-secondary education.

The regional dimension

The experiments we have described often concern fields of interest that are national and international as well as local – for example health, the environment, energy, economics, management, education or industrial technologies. The university cannot limit its horizon to that of the local community. If however we have repeatedly put greater emphasis on the local and regional dimension, it is because it is at its regional level that the optimal utilisation of the resources of the university and those of its environment can be achieved and, above all, because to stress the need for interaction between partners presupposes that it is possible to identify those partners and that there is some kind of balance in the power relationships between them.

Admittedly, different types of higher education institutions do not have the same relationships with their immediate environment. Institutions like the Polytechnics (United Kingdom), the Community and Regional Colleges (United States), the Colleges of Advanced Education (Australia), the Regional Colleges (Norway) tend to be regionally oriented, mainly because of the occupational training and continuing training that they provide in response to local needs, and the applied research that they develop for the benefit of the immediate community. The universities, on the other hand, see themselves in a different context – worldwide or nationwide – the central feature of which is the production of knowledge. Their real environment is the international academic community. It is for that community that they produce, it is by that community that they wish to be judged.

But this dichotomy between responsibilities at local and regional level on the one hand and at national and international level on the other deserves to be looked at more closely, among other things in its function as an ideological mask. It would be as wrong to suggest that a university that responds to its environmental context would in consequence lose its universal significance, as it would be to claim that problem-oriented research is a deviation from fundamental research. In reality, the area of influence of a university depends on the function being considered. If one is thinking primarily of the teaching function, the environment is defined on the basis of the area of recruitment of students on the one hand, and the area over which they will find jobs on the other. If one is thinking primarily of the *research* function – the approach generally adopted by university staff – the environment corresponds to the area over which the research findings may be disseminated, that is to say "a continuum which may range from zero to universal". If, finally, one is thinking primarily of the *service* function, one is inclined to choose a smaller radius of action: that of the commune, or the region, but sometimes nevertheless that of the nation or of an international area for certain specific problems.

There is therefore a great deal to be said for the view expressed by the Trade Union Advisory Committee to the OECD that a delicate balance must be found and maintained between these various local, regional, national, international dimensions, so as to avoid solutions at either extreme – the "parish pump" university, or the university completely cut off from its environment in the name of pure knowledge, the university under the thumb of local dignitaries or the university which is the agent of the centralistic state.

The development of relations with the community thus requires some hard precise thinking about the connections between the local, regional, national and international functions of higher education. *Giving a certain importance to the local, and above all the regional dimension does not mean giving it pride of place, and certainly not limiting the area of influence of the university, but rather drawing attention to the advantages to be gained if the university projects itself through practical interactions with a well-defined environment.*

Building a communication and information system between the university and its environment

We have analysed at length, particularly in Part Two, a number of mechanisms and structures through which the demands of the community are taken into account.

They all show that it is quite out of the question that the government of the university should be solely an internal one. They also show how conflicting people's ideas of the university are, and how little is known of its activities, statutes and procedures. Thus, over and above arrangements for community representation on university bodies, *the search for more systematic information procedures seems to be an essential precondition for the development of university/community relations.*

Many different images of the university are to be found in the community, some of them vastly oversimplified. The working classes may think of it as an élitist institution, the employers as an institution which is not doing its job, the politicians as an institution which meddles in matters that do not concern it. At one and the same time, therefore, the community questions the university's right to look into "outside" affairs and reproaches it for pursuing its own peculiar ends. This unfavourable image is reinforced by the opaqueness of certain university practices: the subtle mechanisms for co-opting staff in some countries, the apparently esoteric nature of certain types of research, the difficulty students have in making the transition from studies to working life – none of these are factors making for mutual esteem.

It would seem that the higher education institutions are trying to make their aims and achievements better known by increasing recourse to the advertising media and the use of journalistic techniques. An opinion survey made in Germany in the summer of 1979, after a campaign of this kind, showed that more than half the persons questioned had confidence in higher education, whereas three years previously a similar majority thought the other way.

In other countries similar efforts have been made to influence the public, employers, or the public authorities. One example of this was the "Science Fair" in Austria, another the attempt of a number of teachers of physics from the French University of Aix-Marseille to present their work to "the man in the streeet".

The Standing Conference of Rectors, Presidents and Vice-Chancellors of European Universities (CRE) put this issue very clearly: "having become one institution among others, the university is in direct competition with other socio-political structures in regard to the interest and needs of public opinion. It therefore has to learn how to present its contribution to the general public so as to convince it of the value of its effort in the development of society and thus justify its claim to taxpayers' money"[44].

Besides dissipating the mystery surrounding certain kinds of university knowledge hitherto regarded as inaccessible, such attempts would seem to be indispensable for establishing more effective relationships in a climate of mutual confidence. Academics often consider that the specialised learned journals and the handbooks addressed to students are adequate ways of telling people what they are doing; in fact, this indifference to the need for information and the absence of any serious thinking about the ultimate purposes of the university are part and parcel of the same attitude. *This concern for informing the public reflects a new definition of the functions and responsibilities of the university.* It also corresponds to the choice of a strategy oriented either towards the public authorities considered as the mediators in any relations with the community, or towards a more direct participation in the activities of that community. Finally, it signifies that the university does not consider that it has a monopoly of the knowledge that it puts at the disposal of the community, and that in volunteering to make its activities and programmes generally known, it recognises the ability of public opinion to make critical judgements without, however, relinquishing its own authority to decide or to propose.

Introducing planned changes in policies for post-secondary education

Within the two broad policy developments just considered, a number of practical objectives (or, indeed, guidelines) can be seen to lie behind the proper realisation of university/community relations and of the socially significant role of higher education:

- Greater harmonization of local and regional development policies and post-secondary education policies, in particular as regards vocational training, employment and research;
- Development of co-ordination between post-secondary education institutions at regional and national levels in order to facilitate the sharing of resources and improve co-operation in all fields – teaching, research and social services – in accordance with the specific qualities and vocations of each. In our studies we have confined ourselves to the universities, but the whole of post-secondary education will be involved in the reorganisation proposed;
- Reorganisation of policies for admission to higher education to facilitate access for new groups, in particular adults with work experience and a considerable knowledge of local problems and needs;
- Reorganisation of the institutional and pedagogical structures of post-secondary education in order to promote in the latter social, economic and cultural missions of an interdisciplinary nature for the benefit of the community;
- Development of research policies aimed at a cross-fertilization between fundamental research and action-oriented research arising out of the major socio-economic problems of the community;
- Introduction of teaching and research personnel policies enabling those engaged in community-oriented actions to enjoy a system of rewards and promotion comparable to that of their colleagues;
- Introduction of an effectively democratic management of higher education institutions including participation of representatives of the community, and the promotion in this context of institutional autonomy in regard to the management and optimal utilisation of available resources including those of the community.

These various points might constitute guidelines for the development of future policies for higher education.

3. A REDEFINITION OF UNIVERSITY AUTONOMY

In the introduction to this report we emphasized that we should be looking mainly at relations between the community and the universities, as distinct from the higher education or the post-secondary system in general. In some chapters, however, we have had to consider higher education institutions as a whole because of the impact that certain changes in the university might have on non-university institutions.

Generally speaking, the latter have less hesitation in developing or reinforcing their links with the community. In the universities, resistance to a further increase in relations with the community is based mainly on the fear that this might bring into question a privilege they have enjoyed throughout their history, namely their autonomy. But discussions of the question of autonomy often get off to a false start because of a twofold confusion of concepts.

The first misunderstanding is to confuse "academic freedom" with the "autonomy" of institutions.

Academic freedom is the freedom of individuals to decide not only what their opinions are but also how they are to be expressed, to choose the subject of their research and their working methods, and in certain cases the way in which their findings are to be disseminated. This academic freedom is in fact an extension of the freedom of any individual in a democratic and pluralist society. It is moreover consubstantial with the spirit of research. Academic freedom as an individual right is in fact rarely contested – explicitly at least – though sometimes there may be a reluctance to provide the concrete means of exercising it. An individual's "academic freedom" is moreover more often limited or blocked by his peers or hierarchical superiors in the university than by pressures exerted by the environment.

University autonomy is an attribute of an institution – an institution which, whatever its status, is providing a public service, and which depends either partially or wholly on public funds. The question of autonomy is often raised in defence of a system of self-government in which no other body is represented or has any decision-making rights. The ultimate authority resides, in the most widespread and historically long-standing case, in the community of professors (often to the exclusion of the other teachers), or in less frequent and more recent cases, in the community of professors, other teachers and students, and sometimes the administrative personnel. An autonomy such as this corresponds much more to the definition of a system of "privileges" than to that of freedom, and is well expressed in the French term "franchises universitaires". These privileges may be accompanied by very weak decision-making powers in the "government" of the universities. All these models are currently to be found in OECD Member countries.

A second confusion arises as between the notions of independence (or rather non-dependence) and autonomy. Independence (or non-dependence) is an essentially relative notion – implying independence in regard to the political authorities, the State, local magnates, various pressures from the environment, and private or public financial interests. The image of the ivory tower – an image both positive (ivory is a precious substance, white (pure?), resistant to time and weather) and negative – expresses this kind of independence very well. One might also use the image of a fortress under siege but protected by a kind of mutual understanding whereby the besiegers recognise that different laws may apply inside the fortress. A fortress however is a place which it is difficult to get into and almost equally difficult to get out of. University independence is usually defended in one of two ways. The first is by the establishment of a more or less implicit agreement of mutual non-intervention whereby the university exchanges a promise of neutrality or of non-commitment (interpreted as the logical consequences of scientific objectivity) against a promise of non-intervention on the part of the community in the internal government of the university, in the orientation of research and in the determination of curricula. The second is by a many-sided search for own resources which serve as a guarantee of internal independence. The latter has always been the way chosen by the private universities, but it is increasingly being adopted by the other institutions as their resources are cut back.

It is possible to give yet other interpretations of university autonomy. It can mean, for example, that the universities have the right themselves to decide a number of questions which, because of their economic and social consequences, are of fundamental importance for the environment too – in particular, rules of entry for students, and procedures for the recruitment of teachers and researchers. It can mean, too, that the university has the right to undertake "initiatives" and "commitments"; in other words it can decide the general direction of its own policies, which may extend over a longer time-scale than the guarantee of public funds that are usually awarded annually; other

155

implications are that it has powers to decide how part of its resources in finance, manpower, and equipment are to be used; or that it can interact with its environment, receiving demands and putting forward proposals. Whichever interpretation may be preferred, the idea was well encapsulated by Mr. O'Keefe (Rapporteur Général of the OECD Intergovernmental Conference on "Policies for Higher Education in the 1980s") in the words: "The traditional autonomy of higher education is seen not as an accident of history but as the necessary condition for a productive and creative enterprise."

All of this (as we have already stressed) adds up to the university's recognition of the demands of the environment, the setting up of effective and multiple mechanisms for interaction, the search for concerted and negotiated procedures for programming on the one hand and, on the other, to its authority to resist, reject, and criticise – an essential condition for the viable development of interactivity with which we are here concerned.

Here again we have support for the contention (which has been building up during the present discussion) that development of relations with the community, far from representing a threat to university autonomy, accepts and reinforces it. At the same time it brings about a shift in emphasis, so that university autonomy implies more the positive ability to be an effective partner with areas of the community than the negative defence of a set of freedoms, recognition of which may take very ambiguous forms. Autonomy cannot be defined as an absence of political, social and economic pressures. It is a whole body of initiatives, with the differing degrees of freedom that such a complex may entail.

So, as we have said, *autonomy is not independence.* Its role is in particular to create conditions for a free circulation of information and critical analysis. To stop that free circulation at the frontiers of the university world would thus be to envisage autonomy as no more than a protective well around the autarky of the university.

What the university can and cannot do

In Chapters 2 and 3 of Part One, we tried to bring out the complexity of the notion of "service" and the ambiguity of "community". The community is not a homogeneous body, it is riven with conflicts, organised in hierarchical structures, and many of its members are simply left out in the cold. This being so, it is important to be clear about what the university can and cannot do and the competencies of the community partners and other types of institution. There should be no question of the university taking over other people's responsibilities. In a national or regional literacy campaign, for example, a university might analyse and assess needs, disseminate information, help to "educate the educators"; but it would not be responsible for carrying out the campaign itself nor indeed would it be capable of doing so. For the university to try and deal with all the problems of the community would not only be impossible materially and economically, it would also be an attempt to reconstitute a form of paternalism and intellectual imperialism which would run counter to any development of relations with the community.

To these difficulties must be added the fact that the idea of *community need* or *demand* is far from clear. The "needs" expressed often reflect interests rather than real needs, and are influenced by what it is thought the university can provide. It is thus necessary to decode the language in which these needs are expressed and analyse them, even if one is not necessarily going to respond to them. This, perhaps, is precisely the kind of specific intervention the university should make. Because it is a place for training and research, and because, as a place for research, it is constantly calling into question any accepted response like any other received truth, the university cannot simply be a supplier of services as ordered. *Our conclusion is, therefore, that unlike a planning office, an industrial research laboratory, or an occupational training centre, the university can,*

*and should, be called upon to pronounce upon the advisability of the demand, the
pertinence of the solutions proposed, and the consequences to be envisaged. This should be
irrespective of who is going to implement them.*

Objectivity, the critical approach and commitment

The development of relations between the university and the community raises a
number of theoretical and policy questions, and also some practical ones. The
theoretical questions concern the *social, cultural and economic responsibility of the
university* in regard to its local, regional and, quite obviously, national and international
environments. That responsibility is closely linked to the questions of academic
objectivity and the critical function, while constituting a permanent challenge to
them.

Theoretically neutral, the university, like justice, is a fragile institution which
largely owes its existence to the desire of the community to have at its disposal an
objective and "absolute" system of reference independent of transitory trends and
influences. At the same time, the universities have throughout their history experienced
considerable pressures from a variety of public, professional or financial bodies who saw
no reason why they should support institutions that they did not completely control and
whose lines of enquiry could lead to a bringing into question of existing values and
activities. In its extreme form the universities' refusal to participate in the conflicts going
on around them came to constitute a political stance which the authorities of the day
found intolerable, and we know how often, up to the end of the 19th century, and even
later in some countries, the universities were temporarily or even permanently closed for
having refused to give their support to this or that dominant group.

Higher education institutions, and particularly the university, stubbornly defend
their neutrality, but subject as they are to financial or political constraints, they do not
find this easy to do. And it becomes even more difficult as soon as they begin to
participate in training for the professions. Indeed, the profiles of the specialists they train
are conditioned by a necessarily transitory and relative state of the economy. The
university sometimes finds that it is in contradiction with itself in on the one hand
pursuing objective enquiries that may perhaps run counter to the present situation, and
on the other hand participating in the maintenance of that situation by the training it
decides to provide without having subjected it to critical appraisal or a sufficiently long
view. The university therefore tends to develop a free zone sheltered from the changing
winds of current opinions, a territory for freedom of expression and an untrammelled
search for truth – whence the temptation, each time the community puts questions to it,
to reply either by neutrality or by refusal.

But to be simply "neutral" is to participate in the values of the system in which one
finds oneself and to protect that system by providing it with new knowledge and
graduates, that is to say with some of the means for maintaining itself. The desire to
develop "service" functions is not therefore a threat to neutrality, but it does reveal its
ambiguities.

As soon as the university decides to engage in analyses of the expectations of the
society that surrounds it, that is to say when it ceases to be solely preoccupied with its
own internal objectives, it becomes a political partner. In doing so it runs the risk of not
sharing some of those expectations, and above all of having to choose between objectives
which it would be illusory to imagine are supported unanimously by all the potential
clients of the university. With the development of relations with the community,
therefore, the question of academic objectivity has fairly and squarely to be faced.

It is wrong to think that objectivity, a critical approach and commitment are
mutually incompatible. Research is always intended to be objective, but its social,
political or economic function depends on the groups that will use the results of that

research in their own interest. In other words, the subject chosen for research acquires importance from the social consequences that the research findings will have when applied. These consequences will be perceived more clearly if the university is in close touch with the community, but they will differ according to the groups within the community with whom the university has established such relations: big industrialists or small working farmers, the regional administration or disadvantaged groups of the population, for example.

For the university, agreeing to enter into relationships with the environment, and choosing to play an explicit role in the way society works, means the following:

- Recognising that it has always had a political function, if only as a consequence of the inequalities in student recruitment, the fact that academics occupy some of the leading positions in society, and its attachment to cultural values, including that of objectivity, which are not necessarily values shared by all social groups;
- Admitting that the university world is itself affected by the decisions, inequalities and conflicts that divide the environment on a variety of issues;
- Giving the university a special mission to promote a given type of social development, and bringing out to the full the link between the critical function and academic objectivity on the one hand and the conception of democracy on the other.

Developing relations with the community: an opportunity or a danger for the university?

The development of relations with the community thus raises a number of serious problems that must be faced. It is also a reminder that, whatever their functions, higher education and research depend for their resources on the community and cannot adopt a stand-offish attitude which is all the more inadmissible because the effect of those activities on the environment and on the development of society may be considerable. By definition, fundamental research is research that has the most numerous applications and the most serious consequences. Can it nonetheless be limited in the name of its possible applications?

The development of relations with the community also entails constraints for the universities.

The first is the obligation they must accept of being accountable to the public authorities and the various partners, and having to justify in increasing detail the way they use the funds they have been granted for their "community related" activities. This is a process that may lead to strict self-censorship with regard to activities the need for which is difficult to justify.

A second constraint is the inevitable tendency further to institutionalise the relations by setting up a variety of administrative bodies both within the university establishment and in the community itself. We have come across quite a number of such offices, committees, and institutes in the course of our enquiry, and they tend to proliferate, leading to a bureaucratisation of relations between the university and the community, under the pretext of strengthening them and making them more systematic. In fact, this tendency could well run counter to the diversity of the ways used by the universities to reduce the risk of conflict between neutrality and commitment by creating an artificial unity of relations in central bodies charged with carrying out a coherent policy. Experience has shown that a certain lack of consistency in attitudes (students taking a different position from their teachers, one department dealing more with enterprises and another more with trade unions) could be a safeguard for university freedom.

A third constraint has to do with the obligation on the university to participate in the laws of the market once it begins to provide services in the sense in which we have defined them. This constraint has been particularly well described by Robert Cottave, General Secretary of the French National Federation of Engineers and Executives, who represented the unions at the Semaine de Bruges on the "University and Society"[13]:

"It is therefore natural that the university should now be seeking to come to terms with the 'outside world', to face up to its existence by conforming to the rules of the market – hence the adoption of terms new to university circles, such as 'client' and 'service' in the narrowest sense. Perhaps that is the way for it to survive, but it will be at the cost of sacrificing the very essence of its function. Indeed, in this 'innovatory' relationship with a 'different clientèle', the university will naturally find itself engaged in the imperturbable mechanisms of the market. It will quickly fall in line with the enterprise model, with its primary aims (to maximise profit), with its automatic reactions, with its values. It will provide its irrefutable guarantees for the quality of growth such as we are currently experiencing. Is it conceivable that in this 'parallel' activity, in this 'new relationship' of supplier to client, the university will be able to propose and impose its basic values by being there to scrutinise, to study, to debate, to understand, to know – values which form the basis of the service the university provides to society?"

Fundamental thinking on university policies is therefore necessary. But we must never lose sight of the fact that the basis of the relationship between the university and society is respect for the special competence of the university, a competence which cannot be defined simply as academic in the sense of the elaboration and production of new knowledge, but which includes a broad cultural element and which is above all based on a fundamental self-questioning about the nature of knowledge itself, about social practices, about collective values [45].

REFERENCES

1. *Innovation in Higher Education: Three German universities,* OECD, 1970.

2. Colloque sur les Contenus et les modalités d'une formation répondant à la demande des sujets collectifs. UNESCO/ED/Conf. 612, Coll. No. 2.

3. "Université, ville et territoire". *Architecture d'Aujourd'hui,* Dossier No. 183, 1976.

4. *Innovation in Higher Education: New universities in the United Kingdom,* OECD, 1969.

5. Quoted by R.G. Forman in "Seminar on Strategies for Developing the Public Image of Higher Education", 7-9 September 1981, OECD/IMHE.

6. Survey carried out from 3 April to 23 May 1980.

7. *Education Record,* Vol. 57, 40.

8. *Applied and public service research in the University of California,* March 1974 and *Academic public service at the University of California,* July 1975.

9. Report of the Committee on the Role of the University of Saskatchewan within the Community, 1975.

10. *Plan for the more effective delivery of extension and continuing education,* March 1977 and *Public service policy statement,* October 1975, Rutgers University at New Brunswick, New Jersey.

11. "The policy analysis role of the contemporary university". Richard F. Ericson in "The Faculty is the heart of the trouble", in *Fortune,* January 1969.

12. *The citizen student.* Canadian Association for University Continuing Education, Toronto, 1977.

13. *Université et société : Le concept de fonction de service public des universités.* Ladislav Cerych. Séminaire de Bruges, Collège de l'Europe, 1973.

14. *A concept paper on public university.* Public Service Agency Educational Cooperation, November 1976.

15. *University-Regional interaction survey.* New York State University, Albany, Spring 1976.

16. "Adaptation de la formation du personnel communal aux mutations des administrations municipales" in *Cahiers de l'Aménagement du Territoire,* Presses Universitaires de Grenoble, 1977.

17. *The foundation for multidisciplinary education in community health,* Adelaide University, Australia, 1977, p. 9.

18. "L'université, les entreprises et la multiplication des salaires bourgeois" in *Actes de la Recherche,* No. 34. Paris, September 1980.

19. "The American university". Jacques Barzum, OUP 1969 and Sir Frazer Noble in "Commonwealth universities in congress: Pressures and priorities". Association of Commonwealth Universities. London, 1979.

20. "Le rôle des universités dans l'éducation ouvrière". ILO, 1975. Proceedings of 1973 Colloquium.

21. On these problems, cf.:
    "The Regional Factor in Economic Development", OECD, June 1970.
    Issues of Regional Policies, by A. Emanuel, OECD, September 1973.
    Regional Problems and Policies in OECD Countries, Vol. 1, May 1976.
    Education and Regional Development, OECD, 1979. Vol. 1: General Report; Vol. 2: Technical Reports.

22. *Re-appraisal of Regional Policies in OECD Countries,* OECD, February 1975.

23. Education and regional development: an overview of a growing controversy", *European Journal of Education,* Vol. 14, No. 3, September 1979.

24. "Possibilités d'une politique européenne de l'université". CRE - Information No. 48, 1979.

25. "L'Enseignement Supérieur en Alternance" par B. Girod de l'Ain. Actes du Colloque national de Rennes. *Documentation Française.* Paris, 1974.

26. *Recurrent Education: Trends and Issues,* OECD, 1975.

27. *Recurrent Education in the 80's: Trends and policies,* not yet published.

28. *Health, Higher Education and the Community: Towards a Regional Health University,* OECD, 1977.

29. *Polytechnics: the shared use of space and facilities.* G. Kenny, Department of Education and Science, September 1977.

30. Cf. OCDE, *International Journal of Institutional Management in Higher Education,* No. 2. Vol. 5, July 1981.

31. *A Strategy for Change in Higher Education: The Extended University of the University of California,* D.P. Gardner and J. Zelan, OECD, 1974.

32. "The Venture Capital of Higher Education. The private and public source of discretionary funds". The Carnegie Council on Policy Studies in Higher Education, 1980.

33. *Structure of Studies and Place of Research in Mass Higher Education,* OECD, 1974.

34. *L'Enseignement Supérieur dans la Région Provence-Alpes-Côte d'Azur,* Experton, Langevin, Reiffers. Université d'Aix-Marseille II, July 1977.

35. "Le Centre Universitaire de Roskilde: une intégration socio-économique d'une innovation au Danemark". *Expériences et Innovation en Éducation,* No. 29. UNESCO-BIE. Paris, 1976.

36. "The Outline of New Town for Education and Research". Institut de recherche sur l'Enseignement Supérieur. Hiroshima University. 1977.

37. *Louvain-la-Neuve. Une ville nouvelle pour une société nouvelle,* Michel Woitrin.

38. M. Weinberg in *Science,* No. 149, 1965.

39. *Interdisciplinarity: Problems of Teaching and Research in Universities,* OECD, 1972.

40. *Environmental Education at University level: Trends and Data.* OECD, 1973.

41. *Environmental Problems and Higher Education,* OECD, 1976.

42. *The Future of University Research,* OECD, 1981.

43. *Technical Change and Economic Policy, Science and Technology in the New Economic and Social Context,* OECD, 1980.

44. CRE Information, No. 53, 1st quarter, Geneva.

45. Cf. Université: Fécondité d'une crise, in *Esprit.* November/December 1978. No. 11-12.

OECD SALES AGENTS
DÉPOSITAIRES DES PUBLICATIONS DE L'OCDE

ARGENTINA – ARGENTINE
Carlos Hirsch S.R.L., Florida 165, 4° Piso (Galería Guemes)
1333 BUENOS AIRES, Tel. 33.1787.2391 y 30.7122
AUSTRALIA – AUSTRALIE
Australia and New Zealand Book Company Pty, Ltd.,
10 Aquatic Drive, Frenchs Forest, N.S.W. 2086
P.O. Box 459, BROOKVALE, N.S.W. 2100
AUSTRIA – AUTRICHE
OECD Publications and Information Center
4 Simrockstrasse 5300 BONN. Tel. (0228) 21.60.45
Local Agent/Agent local :
Gerold and Co., Graben 31, WIEN 1. Tel. 52.22.35
BELGIUM – BELGIQUE
LCLS
35, avenue de Stalingrad, 1000 BRUXELLES. Tel. 02.512.89.74
BRAZIL – BRÉSIL
Mestre Jou S.A., Rua Guaipa 518,
Caixa Postal 24090, 05089 SAO PAULO 10. Tel. 261.1920
Rua Senador Dantas 19 s/205-6, RIO DE JANEIRO GB.
Tel. 232.07.32
CANADA
Renouf Publishing Company Limited,
2182 St. Catherine Street West,
MONTRÉAL, Que. H3H 1M7. Tel. (514)937.3519
OTTAWA, Ont. K1P 5A6, 61 Sparks Street
DENMARK – DANEMARK
Munksgaard Export and Subscription Service
35, Nørre Søgade
DK 1370 KØBENHAVN K. Tel. +45.1.12.85.70
FINLAND – FINLANDE
Akateeminen Kirjakauppa
Keskuskatu 1, 00100 HELSINKI 10. Tel. 65.11.22
FRANCE
Bureau des Publications de l'OCDE,
2 rue André-Pascal, 75775 PARIS CEDEX 16. Tel. (1) 524.81.67
Principal correspondant :
13602 AIX-EN-PROVENCE : Librairie de l'Université.
Tel. 26.18.08
GERMANY – ALLEMAGNE
OECD Publications and Information Center
4 Simrockstrasse 5300 BONN Tel. (0228) 21.60.45
GREECE – GRÈCE
Librairie Kauffmann, 28 rue du Stade,
ATHÈNES 132. Tel. 322.21.60
HONG-KONG
Government Information Services,
Publications/Sales Section, Baskerville House,
2/F., 22 Ice House Street
ICELAND – ISLANDE
Snaebjörn Jönsson and Co., h.f.,
Hafnarstraeti 4 and 9, P.O.B. 1131, REYKJAVIK.
Tel. 13133/14281/11936
INDIA – INDE
Oxford Book and Stationery Co. :
NEW DELHI-1, Scindia House. Tel. 45896
CALCUTTA 700016, 17 Park Street. Tel. 240832
INDONESIA – INDONÉSIE
PDIN-LIPI, P.O. Box 3065/JKT., JAKARTA, Tel. 583467
IRELAND – IRLANDE
TDC Publishers – Library Suppliers
12 North Frederick Street, DUBLIN 1 Tel. 744835-749677
ITALY – ITALIE
Libreria Commissionaria Sansoni :
Via Lamarmora 45, 50121 FIRENZE. Tel. 579751
Via Bartolini 29, 20155 MILANO. Tel. 365083
Sub-depositari :
Editrice e Libreria Herder,
Piazza Montecitorio 120, 00 186 ROMA. Tel. 6794628
Libreria Hoepli, Via Hoepli 5, 20121 MILANO. Tel. 865446
Libreria Lattes, Via Garibaldi 3, 10122 TORINO. Tel. 519274
La diffusione delle edizioni OCSE è inoltre assicurata dalle migliori
librerie nelle città più importanti.
JAPAN – JAPON
OECD Publications and Information Center,
Landic Akasaka Bldg., 2-3-4 Akasaka,
Minato-ku, TOKYO 107 Tel. 586.2016
KOREA – CORÉE
Pan Korea Book Corporation,
P.O. Box n° 101 Kwangwhamun, SÉOUL. Tel. 72.7369
LEBANON – LIBAN
Documenta Scientifica/Redico,
Edison Building, Bliss Street, P.O. Box 5641, BEIRUT.
Tel. 354429 – 344425

MALAYSIA – MALAISIE
and/et SINGAPORE - SINGAPOUR
University of Malaysia Co-operative Bookshop Ltd.
P.O. Box 1127, Jalan Pantai Baru
KUALA LUMPUR. Tel. 51425, 54058, 54361
THE NETHERLANDS – PAYS-BAS
Staatsuitgeverij
Verzendboekhandel Chr. Plantijnstraat 1
Postbus 20014
2500 EA S-GRAVENHAGE. Tel. nr. 070.789911
Voor bestellingen: Tel. 070.789208
NEW ZEALAND – NOUVELLE-ZÉLANDE
Publications Section,
Government Printing Office Bookshops:
AUCKLAND: Retail Bookshop: 25 Rutland Street,
Mail Orders: 85 Beach Road, Private Bag C.P.O.
HAMILTON: Retail Ward Street,
Mail Orders, P.O. Box 857
WELLINGTON: Retail: Mulgrave Street (Head Office),
Cubacade World Trade Centre
Mail Orders: Private Bag
CHRISTCHURCH: Retail: 159 Hereford Street,
Mail Orders: Private Bag
DUNEDIN: Retail: Princes Street
Mail Order: P.O. Box 1104
NORWAY – NORVÈGE
J.G. TANUM A/S Karl Johansgate 43
P.O. Box 1177 Sentrum OSLO 1. Tel. (02) 80.12.60
PAKISTAN
Mirza Book Agency, 65 Shahrah Quaid-E-Azam, LAHORE 3.
Tel. 66839
PHILIPPINES
National Book Store, Inc.
Library Services Division, P.O. Box 1934, MANILA.
Tel. Nos. 49.43.06 to 09, 40.53.45, 49.45.12
PORTUGAL
Livraria Portugal, Rua do Carmo 70-74,
1117 LISBOA CODEX. Tel. 360582/3
SPAIN – ESPAGNE
Mundi-Prensa Libros, S.A.
Castelló 37, Apartado 1223, MADRID-1. Tel. 275.46.55
Libreria Bosch, Ronda Universidad 11, BARCELONA 7.
Tel. 317.53.08, 317.53.58
SWEDEN – SUÈDE
AB CE Fritzes Kungl Hovbokhandel,
Box 16 356, S 103 27 STH, Regeringsgatan 12,
DS STOCKHOLM. Tel. 08/23.89.00
SWITZERLAND – SUISSE
OECD Publications and Information Center
4 Simrockstrasse 5300 BONN. Tel. (0228) 21.60.45
Local Agents/Agents locaux
Librairie Payot, 6 rue Grenus, 1211 GENÈVE 11. Tel. 022.31.89.50
Freihofer A.G., Weinbergstr. 109, CH-8006 ZÜRICH.
Tel. 01.3634282
TAIWAN – FORMOSE
Good Faith Worldwide Int'l Co., Ltd.
9th floor, No. 118, Sec. 2
Chung Hsiao E. Road
TAIPEI. Tel. 391.7396/391.7397
THAILAND – THAILANDE
Suksit Siam Co., Ltd., 1715 Rama IV Rd,
Samyan, BANGKOK 5. Tel. 2511630
TURKEY – TURQUIE
Kültur Yayinlari Is-Türk Ltd. Sti.
Atatürk Bulvari No : 77/B
KIZILAY/ANKARA. Tel. 17 02 66
Dolmabahce Cad. No : 29
BESIKTAS/ISTANBUL. Tel. 60 71 88
UNITED KINGDOM – ROYAUME-UNI
H.M. Stationery Office, P.O.B. 569,
LONDON SE1 9NH. Tel. 01.928.6977, Ext. 410 or
49 High Holborn, LONDON WC1V 6 HB (personal callers)
Branches at: EDINBURGH, BIRMINGHAM, BRISTOL,
MANCHESTER, CARDIFF, BELFAST.
UNITED STATES OF AMERICA – ÉTATS-UNIS
OECD Publications and Information Center, Suite 1207,
1750 Pennsylvania Ave., N.W. WASHINGTON, D.C.20006 – 4582
Tel. (202) 724.1857
VENEZUELA
Libreria del Este, Avda. F. Miranda 52, Edificio Galipan,
CARACAS 106. Tel. 32.23.01/33.26.04/33.24.73
YUGOSLAVIA – YOUGOSLAVIE
Jugoslovenska Knjiga, Terazije 27, P.O.B. 36, BEOGRAD.
Tel. 621.992

Les commandes provenant de pays où l'OCDE n'a pas encore désigné de dépositaire peuvent être adressées à :
OCDE, Bureau des Publications, 2, rue André-Pascal, 75775 PARIS CEDEX 16.

Orders and inquiries from countries where sales agents have not yet been appointed may be sent to:
OECD, Publications Office, 2 rue André-Pascal, 75775 PARIS CEDEX 16.

65432-7-1982

OECD PUBLICATIONS, 2, rue André-Pascal, 75775 PARIS CEDEX 16 - No. 42149 1982
PRINTED IN FRANCE
(96 82 02 1) ISBN 92-64-12370-9